Praise for *The Dangerous Act of Loving Your Neighbor*

"Mark Labberton draws us to understand the reality of injustice in our world—a reality that we can all too easily turn into vague abstractions—by beginning first with a raw, honest examination of our own hearts. Mark's manner with his reader is at the same time gracious and incisive, invoking careful consideration of the assumptions and broken perceptions that lead us away from the heart of God—and above all, compelling us to a restored perception of the image of God in every human being. This is a book you will want to spend considerable time ingesting, and as you do so, you are sure to be changed. Let this book lead you to encounter the gospel from a renewed perspective, bringing you into a transformed relationship with the broken world that God has called his people to love with justice."

GARY A. HAUGEN, president and CEO, International Justice Mission, and author of *The Good News About Injustice*

"*The Dangerous Act of Loving Your Neighbor* is a book that I've been waiting for! It is a practical and thought-provoking guide that shows us how to cultivate lives of justice, mercy and faith in a world that is in desperate need of compassion and reconciliation. I highly recommend this book to everyone who really wants to make a difference in the world. It is an outstanding sequel to *The Dangerous Act of Worship!*"

Rev. Dr. Brenda Salter McNeil, president, Salter McNeil & Associates, and author of *The Heart of Racial Justice*

"Mark Labberton's new book, *The Dangerous Act of Loving Your Neighbor,* is an intensely human and courageously confessional reflection on radical loving. His pastoral approach is inviting, drawing the reader into the urgent conversation that thoughtful Christians need as they desperately attempt to reclaim an embodied love in a world that longs to experience it. Provocative, prophetic, pastoral and passionate about living into a reality of love, Mark's book is captivating and compelling."

Chris Heuertz, international director, Word Made Flesh, author of *Simple Spirituality* and coauthor of *Friendship at the Margins*

"Reading Mark Labberton's book . . . has rekindled my faith in the gospel of Jesus—the good news of God, who sees, names and acts truly, in love; a gospel that frees me to act, without deception or pressure to change anyone. *The Dangerous Act of Loving Your Neighbor* has also rekindled my resolve to continue on the path of seeking God, who alone is just and changes the human heart—my heart, which, except for his grace, is prone to misperceiving, misnaming and misacting! . . . It is groundbreaking in its elucidation of how the roots of injustice are embedded in the shaping of the human heart through the most ordinary stuff of daily human interaction."

Dr. David Zac Niringiye, bishop in the Church of Uganda (Anglican)

"*The Dangerous Act of Loving Your Neighbor* asks important questions, deeper questions we may not have thought to ask yet in our pursuit of justice, and ones that will take a lifetime to answer. We say we want justice, but our self-centric hearts betray us. So how do we override our hearts? This book opened my eyes to the difference between doing something, and becoming *someone*—a person of justice, reoriented to the heart of Jesus."

Sara Groves, singer/songwriter

"Here is a book to heal the demonic split between private religion and public action. Eloquent and subversive, intelligent and passionate, these reflections are designed to move you toward a true worship of God that involves loving him in and through every sphere and domain of life."

Alan Hirsch, author of *The Forgotten Ways* and coauthor (with Debra Hirsch) of *Untamed*

"For too long we have divorced the quest for 'being spiritual' from a commitment to 'doing justice.' In this powerfully inspiring book, Mark Labberton provides wise insights—and some wonderful stories!—about how to connect inside with outside in the Christian life. A must-read for all who care about faithful discipleship!"

Richard J. Mouw, president and professor of Christian philosophy, Fuller Theological Seminary, and author of *Uncommon Decency*

Mark Labberton

The Dangerous Act of

Loving Your Neighbor

Seeing Others Through the Eyes of Jesus

IVP Books

An imprint of InterVarsity Press
Downers Grove, Illinois

InterVarsity Press
P.O. Box 1400, Downers Grove, IL 60515-1426
World Wide Web: www.ivpress.com
Email: email@ivpress.com

InterVarsity Press® is the book-publishing division of InterVarsity Christian Fellowship/USA®,
a movement of students and faculty active on campus at hundreds of universities, colleges and
schools of nursing in the United States of America, and a member movement of the International
Fellowship of Evangelical Students. For information about local and regional activities, write
Public Relations Dept., InterVarsity Christian Fellowship/USA, 6400 Schroeder Rd., P.O. Box
7895, Madison, WI 53707-7895, or visit the IVCF website at <www.intervarsity.org>.

While all stories in this book are true, some names and identifying information have been changed
to protect the privacy of the individuals involved.

Design: Cindy Kiple
Images: Diana Ong/Getty Images

ISBN 978-0-8308-3840-0

Printed in Canada ∞

Library of Congress Cataloging-in-Publication Data

Labberton, Mark, 1953-
  The dangerous act of loving your neighbor: seeing others through
the eyes of Jesus / Mark Labberton.
    p. cm.
  Includes bibliographical references.
  ISBN 978-0-8308-3840-0 (hardcover: alk. paper)
  1. Love—Religious aspects—Christianity. 2. Christian
life—Presbyterian authors. I. Title.
  BV4639.L26 2010
  241'.677—dc22

                                                                    2010024966

P	18	17	16	15	14	13	12	11	10	9	8	7	6	5	4	3	2	1
Y	25	24	23	22	21	20	19	18	17	16	15	14	13	12	11	10		

Dedicated to

Janet, Peter and Sam

Whose hearts have ever changed and enlarged my own

The outward work will never be puny if the inward work is great. And the outward work can never be great or even good if the inward work is puny or of little worth. The inward work invariably includes in itself all breadth, all expansiveness, all length, all depth. Such a work receives and draws all its being from nowhere else except from and in the heart of God.

—MEISTER ECKHART

Contents

Introduction

The Injustice of the Heart

Doris explained that she would have had the muffins there, but she had been kidnapped.

That morning, Doris had parked in her usual spot adjacent to our church in Berkeley and was reaching back inside her car for her basket of oatmeal muffins. As she leaned in, she was powerfully struck from behind and pushed back into the car and across the console into the passenger side. Breathless, a young man jumped into the driver's seat and took off, with Doris riding shotgun. That Doris was in her early eighties, and had had her elegant silver-blonde hair done as usual at 11:00 on Friday, didn't matter at that moment. Suddenly everything changed.

I made my way straight from church to her tidy apartment. Shaken but steady, Doris greeted me at the door. Every protective pastoral corpuscle was firing in me as I leaped at the chance to surround Doris with love and support in the midst of this trauma. But that day, as other times too, Doris proved to be my pastor more than I could be hers.

"After he took off in the car, the first thing I did, of course, was to ask him his name," Doris said. *Of course,* I thought. *When mugged and kidnapped, start by asking for your attacker's name.* "He said it was Jesse," she went on. "So I said, 'Jesse, what are you doing?'

"'I'm kidnapping you so we can go to your ATM and get money out of your account,' Jesse told me.

"So I said, 'Jesse, why are you doing this?'

"He told me it was because he needed the money for drugs. He was addicted and needed a hit. So I just said, 'Well, Jesse, it's a terrible thing to be a drug addict. You really shouldn't be a drug addict. It's not the way you should be living your life.'" *When being kidnapped,* I reflected, *at least make the conversation an honest one.*

By then, Doris explained, they had arrived at the first ATM machine, and after intimidating her for the password, Jesse jumped out to get the cash. As he sped away to the next branch, Doris said she explained to Jesse that he really needed help, that this drug problem was much bigger than he was. He needed help from God, who really loved and understood him. After the next branch stop, Doris told Jesse he also needed an effective drug rehab program. Jesse replied he had tried that, but Doris suggested he needed a better program than the one he described to her. Then she continued, "Jesse, God wants to help you."

By the third bank stop, Jesse had hit the daily withdrawal limit for Doris's account. Since she was no longer useful to him, he pulled the car to the side of the street and explained he was going to leave her there. He had what he needed, he said. But Doris was not done. "Jesse, I am going to pray that you get caught for this, because it's wrong and you shouldn't get away with doing this to people. I'm also going to pray that you will be caught so I can not only testify you did it, but so I can plead with the judge to get you into a really good drug rehab program. You need to get caught, so you can be stopped and helped. You need God to give you the strength to get off drugs and have a better life." *I'm sure I would have said something just like this to a kidnapper.*

"Jesse was just going to leave me there, but I couldn't get out of the car because I was so battered and stiff. So Jesse said he would come around to the other side and help me, which I really appreciated. He came around, opened the door, helped me out, held my arm so I could get to the driver's side and then gave me his arm so I could get into the car. Then he put the seatbelt across me, leaned in and kissed me on the cheek.

"So that's what happened," Doris said.

Pastoral adrenaline still rushing, I leaned toward her and with all the empathy I could exude, I said, "I am so sorry this horrible thing happened, Doris."

"It's true, it is horrible," Doris agreed. But then, without much of a pause, she added, "But the really horrible thing is Jesse's addiction to drugs."

"But it's awful that you should get attacked and kidnapped like this," I responded.

"Well, yes, but really, why not me?" asked Doris. "This sort of thing happens every day to thousands of people. There's no particular reason this shouldn't happen to me."

"Um . . . yes," I stammered.

When Doris finally said, "Let's pray for my getting over this, but also for Jesse," I was thinking that I was also in need of prayer as I tried to absorb this conversation.

It wasn't a great surprise that within a couple of months, Doris was at the police station identifying Jesse. Soon after that, she sat in the witness box at the courthouse: "Yes, hello, Jesse, remember me? Doris? I said I was going to pray for this moment and I told you why. Here we are! Yes, Judge, Jesse was the one, and yes, he did do all those things. And, another thing, Judge, Jesse really needs a good drug rehab program so he can get his life back. I know he's guilty. But he also really needs help, please, Judge."

Doris loved her enemy. She loved her enemy without hesitancy, and she did so in ways that reflect the purpose of her life and the reality of the world she lives in. She did not choose to claim or shrink into victimhood, though she had been violated. She was courageous and honest. She was not in denial. She was willing and able to step toward her enemy with truth and justice, to seek what was best for his welfare without disregarding her own. Everything in Doris believed her God was God for Jesse too. The same love God extended to her was also for him. God's heart seeks the welfare of his enemies, so hers did too.

In the following months I often thought during my times with Doris that my life would be a whole lot more like Jesus' if I could only remember to ask, W.W.D.D. (What Would Doris Do)? That would lead me to a very different life, and almost certainly one a whole lot more filled with the instincts and actions of the One I claim to follow. It would be a story of gaining a different heart, with a different capacity and readiness to respond to a world of injustice and suffering.

INJUSTICE AND THE HEART

This book explores a simple premise: human hearts form the seedbed from which injustice thrives.

Injustice cannot be understood without taking into account systemic realities greater than human hearts and elements beyond individual will. But systemic injustice thrives as it does because human hearts accommodate and allow it. "All that is necessary for evil to triumph is for good men [and women] to do nothing," Edmund Burke said. Most of us have hearts that lead us to do just that.

Some hearts belong to deliberate perpetrators of injustice and suffering. Their hearts *will* the tyranny and oppression they mete out. Contemporary slave owners are among such people. So are child sex-traffickers. Leaders, political and social, often prey on the weak. Bullies thrive everywhere, especially where there is gain with no accountability. This is part of the seedbed from which injustice thrives. But such virulent hearts are not what I am primarily thinking about here.

On the other end of the spectrum are hearts that have been deeply injured as victims of injustice. Possibly you, and certainly many others, are among those who know by personal experience what it means to have suffered as a consequence of others' actions, affecting you perhaps every day in your capacity to function, let alone love. Common injustices like being raised in an alcoholic home, or being physically or sexually abused, can undo lives at a basic level and disable people's capacity to let their hearts be touched or available to respond to the needs of others.

Here we are primarily focusing not on the hearts of heinous perpetrators, nor on the hearts of brutalized victims. Instead, we are focusing on the ordinary heart: the relatively healthy, capable but disconnected hearts of so many. Like me. Like you.

Our hearts don't consciously will injustice. Nor do they deliberately withhold compassion. Nor is it that tales of injustice fail to grab and concern us. Yet our hearts are weak and confused. Our hearts are easily overwhelmed and self-protective. They are prone to be absorbed mostly with the immediacy of our own lives. Our hearts have the capacity to seek justice, but they are usually not calibrated to do so—at least not beyond concern for our inner circle. In a world of such hearts, virulent injustice thrives. Systemic injustice, the absence of the rule of law, and the suffering of so many innocents at the hands of oppressors rely on the complicity and distraction of our ordinary hearts.

Our hearts seem benign, but the situation is more complex than that. Although our hearts may not lead us to will injustice, neither are they healthy and strong enough to drive us to seek justice. That is, we don't have hearts that actively, courageously will and pursue justice, not even for the truly vulnerable. Our hearts do demonstrate our capacity to be determined and focused enough to will some things for ourselves and those we love most: prosperity, education, comfort, safety. For most of us, however, our hearts don't carry a sustained longing for and commitment to justice, for a world of rightly ordered power in which far more people can survive and maybe even thrive.

What this means in spiritual terms, then, is that our hearts thwart God's heart for justice. The One who made us for a loving and just relationship with God, with ourselves, and with one another also gave us the freedom not to love. Many of us think we are simply choosing to live in between the two options, passively letting the pieces fall where they will. But the net result when good people do nothing is that injustice thrives. And most of us have little or no sense of complicity. Even our apparent experience of the Christian faith may not expose the underlying illusion that we are all people with "good hearts."

JESUS AND THE DONKEY

I hope this book reaches deeply into our interior lives, not primarily for our sake, but for the public and personal welfare of others around us and throughout the world. It provides a chance to reflect on why our ordinary hearts can be such a seedbed for injustice, why we can know about injustice but be so complacent about it, and how this can change.

Why don't more of us live like Doris? Is it that we don't have a heart like hers? To live that way, you and I would have to be changed. We, and our world, need that, urgently. Lives depend on it.

To explain what I mean, let's begin with my favorite starting point: myself. I woke this morning to my world, again. It's by no means a perfect world, but it is one with many happy things: love, health, work, comfort. I thank God for these daily graces. I will see and engage the world today, as I have for my adult life, through a series of lenses that include such things as being tall, white, male, educated and well paid. I have other lenses too, of course, being from a particular family, born and raised in Washington State, married with two sons, a Presbyterian pastor and, more recently, a seminary professor. Then there are my personality, my attractions, my contortions, my fears: a world of my own peculiarities that shapes how I see and engage with others—or not. All this constitutes what I call my heart. Mine is the heart of someone who lives a privileged life with more personal, economic and professional power than probably 99 percent of the world.

Now, I can easily think that this is all just me. But, in fact, this "me" only lives and moves and has its being within a complex social system. Many of the basic assumptions of my daily life that I suppose to be distinctly me or mine are actually part of a social context that is anything but simple or neutral. I am what we all are: social beings whose lives reflect, for better and for worse, the social realities we have encountered or that have encountered us. We think our hearts are just our own construction. But our hearts are shaped by the cultural and social assumptions around and within them. We hold all of this in our hearts, and our hearts reflect both our own story and our collected stories.

In this metaphorical sense, our hearts are that vortex of personal and social perceptions and commitments that constitutes how we see, think, feel and respond to life. We commonly refer to this as our "heart" because we are talking about something that seems so central to our life: intimate, powerful, emotional, vulnerable, defining. Wherever we are and whatever we are seeing and doing, our hearts respond to and shape what happens.

This may be fine if my heart matters only to me. But it turns out that it doesn't. My heart is actually of immense interest to God, and to my neighbor. Our hearts have been made to love God and to love our neighbor. That's why we are given the powers of our hearts: to love, to serve and to do justice. These are the most important things about my heart—and mine doesn't do any of them very well. Nor, as it turns out, do most others. The fallout of our selfish hearts lies behind the history of so much war, suffering, injustice and pain.

God, our neighbor and we ourselves all suffer in part because our hearts fail. That's why we urgently need new ones.

When our youngest son, Sam, was four, I was reading him a children's book about Jesus' entry into Jerusalem on a donkey. As we finished reading, Sam gently stroked the cover of the book with its picture of Jesus on the donkey's back. Then, putting his hand to his chest he said to me, "Daddy, Jesus is in my heart."

"Sam, I am so glad you know that," I replied.

He continued feeling his chest rather quizzically as he asked, "But where's the donkey?"

"Trust me, Sam, the donkey is there too . . . the ass is always at hand!" We may or may not have Jesus in our heart, but even if we do, we also have the donkey (see Romans 7). We all know the donkey of resistance, of prejudice, of self-absorption. It's part of the heart problem we share, and most of the time, it's not cute, let alone just or life-giving. This book takes defeating the donkey seriously. The dangerous acts of loving God and our neighbor demand and require it.

WHAT THIS BOOK IS NOT

Before going on, let me be clear about what I am not saying. These convictions about our hearts are not, for example, targeted to induce guilt. I know that is easily possible. I have heard such words, and I've probably preached them. But when guilt is the primary outcome sought, it can come closer to killing our hearts than transforming them, and the latter is the only option that will do any good. The point of a self-examined life is not itself alone. Rather, if self-examination unfolds by the power, grace and wisdom of the Spirit of Jesus Christ, the fruit it bears should be evident in the love and justice toward others that it fosters in the real world. That is where I hope the reflections in this book lead.

I will also not be saying that a simplistic and direct causal relationship exists between every victim's experience of injustice and every other human heart, especially the negligent ones. That would be ludicrous, unbearable and indefensible, besides being untrue. It's the fatal flaw in the "eat your peas because there are starving children in Africa" argument that desperate parents sometimes employ. That perspective simplistically overloads individual responsibility so as to push any thinking person into the fetal position. It defeats responding at all through a kind of overwhelmed paralysis that suggests if you cannot do everything to help, then you cannot do anything to help, and that any act that is not other-centered is self-indulgent. This cripples our hearts rather than freeing them as God intends.

No doubt systemic, social and political elements are pervasively at work in our world, and injustice emerges amid that swirl of influences. I strongly believe in the importance of sophisticated social sciences (such as sociology, economics and political science) in analyzing and advocating social change. That is not what I will be doing in this book, but I assume their vital contribution. What I am writing will be admittedly more pastoral and theological instead, which I hope can be seen as complementary to the task of the social and political sciences.

I am not trying to suggest that injustice in the world can be addressed only by considering the role of an individual heart, or even collective hearts, isolated from their contexts. We are inextricably social creatures, and any adequate explanation of self emerges in part from the ways our social settings set the possibilities for our understanding. I believe the self and society are mutually constitutive. So I am not a social constructivist who believes that the self is a pure social fabrication any more than I am a believer in a naive, autonomous individualism. I will be focusing on the self in a social context and will seek to hold the individual and the social setting in constant, interactive tension.

I will also not be arguing that a change in hearts is the only solution necessary for a socially just world. The Bible itself gives more than ample evidence of the naiveté of such an idea. Scripture makes clear what my own human experience confirms: nothing in the whole world is harder or more important to change at a fundamental level than the human heart (Gen 3; Rom 3). If our personal and historical experience haven't already taught this to us, the cross and resurrection of Jesus Christ should make it plain. Human beings do not readily change. To do that required the greatest divine sacrifice (Matthew 28; John 21; Romans 5; Ephesians 2). And still such a price by no means automatically translates into changed hearts that seek and do justice. Remember: Jesus and the donkey are in our hearts. That's a problem which only God can ultimately change.

POWER, JUSTICE AND INJUSTICE

What are the meanings of *power, justice* and *injustice* as used in this book? The primary Christian confession of faith that "Jesus is Lord" means that the reign of Jesus over all things recasts power in any and all places. No one and nothing else is Lord: neither economic power nor powerlessness, neither political power nor powerlessness, neither class power nor powerlessness. Under the just and loving reign of Jesus, all power is and will be redefined in light of the saving and re-creating power of the One before whom every knee will bow. Injustice at its core always involves the abuse of power. Justice is the right ordering of power. To call Jesus Lord means bringing all of our lives and world before the One who as Lord reorders power and asks us to follow him in doing so. The first and second commandments call God's people to practice using our life's powers to do two central things: to "love the Lord your God with all your heart, and with all your soul, and with all your strength, and with all your mind," and to "love your neighbor as yourself." If we actually seek to do this, it changes our understanding of why and how power and injustice matter, and compels us to live lives that reorder power according to the loving and re-creating reign of Jesus.

CHANGING THE HEART

What I will argue in this book is that, in a complicated world of profound injustice, the crisis of the human heart is crucial to social transformation. Changing our world depends on changing our hearts: how we *perceive*, *name* and *act* in the world. The ways of the heart are reflected in the world daily in how we perceive (see and assess one another), how we name (frame and position one another) and how we act (engage or distance one another). These three are inseparable, simultaneous but distinguishable, and they are a potent force.

Political, social and economic changes are critical. Law and the rule of law are fundamental needs. Especially in a world where the human heart is so bent in on itself, external, public and systemic structures must be brought to bear in service of the most vulnerable. And (not but) within, under, around and through all these will be individuals and societies in whose hearts there needs to be significant changes if the systemic change is going to be sustainable and substantial.

This is the way Martin Luther King Jr. put it when he spoke to the Southern Christian Leadership Conference in Atlanta on August 16, 1967:

> If you will let me be a preacher just a little bit—one night, a juror came to Jesus and he wanted to know what he could do to be saved. Jesus didn't get bogged down in the kind of isolated approach of what he shouldn't do. Jesus didn't say, "Now Nicodemus, you must stop lying." He didn't say, "Nicodemus, you must stop cheating if you are doing that." He didn't say, "Nicodemus, you must not commit adultery." He didn't say, "Nicodemus, now you must stop drinking liquor if you are doing that excessively." He said something altogether different, because Jesus realized something basic—that if a man will lie, he will steal. And if a man will steal, he will kill. So instead of just getting bogged down in

one thing, Jesus looked at him and said, "Nicodemus, you must be born again."

He said, in other words, "Your whole structure must be changed." A nation that will keep people in slavery for 244 years will "thingify" them—make them things. Therefore they will exploit them, and poor people generally, economically. And a nation that will exploit economically will have to have foreign investments and everything else, and will have to use its military might to protect them. All of these problems are tied together. What I am saying today is that we must go from this convention and say, "America, you must be born again!"

What Dr. King was saying, echoing Jesus, and what I want to say, is that in a world filled with suffering and injustice, the transformation needed has to reach all the way into our hearts, behind and underneath systems and structures, laws, and habits: "your whole [personal and social] structure must be changed."

It is ironic that in more recent years in American political rhetoric, "born again" language (Jn 3) has seemed to many like an individualistic appliqué to the surface of social need rather than an invitation to profound transformation for the sake of social change, as Dr. King used it. Of course, most injustice shows itself in public, and as Dr. King knew so well, injustice arises out of the heart. By all and every means public efforts must be marshaled to address the manifold dimensions of social injustice. As that happens, the factor most uniquely addressed by the Christian faith is the core of the problem: the human heart that must be made new so that the world might be made new. People suffer daily around the world because human hearts are unchanged. The practical and tragic consequences continue endlessly.

Meanwhile, much written about the heart in popular Christian literature has little or nothing to do with our public lives, nor with how our public lives ever get connected to what is happening in our hearts. This reflects a false dichotomy between our personal and public selves, rather than reflecting what the Bible sees as the inevitable, comprehensive unity of our lives as persons in community. Loving God must involve loving our neighbor. Or we are not loving God. Read 1 John.

Changing the heart is dramatic. Not just tampering with it, modifying it slightly or redirecting it a bit, but making the heart new and just. That, the Bible says, only God can do. If the God made known in Jesus Christ is doing the work, however, then a comprehensive transformation will be the outcome. Though we cannot readily or finally change ourselves, we can make choices, opening ourselves to the changed heart God wants us to experience. This is a distinctly Christian vocation. The inner, personal work of the grace of Jesus Christ is meant to show itself in the public lives of those who are Christ's disciples. The litmus test is not just how we respond to those who love us, but how we respond to the poor and needy and, even beyond that, to our enemies.

TURNING ON MORE THAN A DIME

I write about this journey of transformation as one who has been on it for many years and who pursues it every day—and who still has a long way to go. Though my life has many happy elements, especially of family and friends, I whine with the best of them on some days: measuring what I don't have, what I wish for, what seems absent or difficult. I am still far too absorbed with myself. I know that song in so many verses and tempos. But when those mesmerizing rhythms are less in control, I am able to hear and even identify with the cries of others, including the empathetic cries of Jesus. Then I know my heart must change, although it is daunting to consider how.

The longer I have lived, the more privileged I have become. I remember many years ago when I realized that as a disciple this was a genuine problem. It has been. It still is. The privilege of my life can move me in the opposite direction from following Jesus' self-emptying example. This is my own personal version of the Constantinian problem that the church and disciples through the ages have often had to face: the more the gospel is aligned with power and its privileges, the more likely it is that the gospel will accommodate itself to the privilege and power rather than the other way around. All this has been the temptation, even as I have been more and more convinced of the self-emptying call of Jesus on my life. I have seen this same dilemma in the lives of many "good-hearted" disciples.

I am only too near the starting point. The happy world of me is just beginning to awaken to the empathy and compassion, justice and love for which I have been made. I am not where I want to be. But I am also not where I was. Some people may come to a transformed heart more easily, but I know that no one has arrived. I am grateful for others far ahead of me in this journey whose hearts and actions more responsibly engage in doing justice one day at a time.

As a pastor, a theologian, a disciple, a global citizen, I am challenged by the daily urgency of a deeper change of heart. Why does the church of Jesus Christ live so complacently in a world where each year nearly eight million children die before the age of five, or where nearly a million children are sold into sex-trafficking? Why, if God is all-good and all-powerful, is the church so unchanged, so untransformed? Why, for example, in a recent study by the Pew Foundation, were white American evangelical Christians the ones who were the most likely to affirm the use of torture in order to gain information from enemies?[1] The heart is hard to change. The heart is the heart of the matter.

ON READING THIS BOOK
Why read this book? I believe it is for your sake and for the sake of

---

[1] Adelle M. Banks, "Poll Shows Support for Torture Among Southern Evangelicals," The Pew Forum on Religion & Public Life, September 11, 2008 <http://pewforum.org/Religion-News/Poll-shows-support-for-torture-among-Southern-evangelicals.aspx>.

others whose lives depend on you and me being changed. For this transformation to occur in concrete terms, we will grapple with the three convergent distortions that arise out of our hearts: *perceiving*, *naming* and *acting*. Distortions intrinsic to these acts constitute the seedbed that allows injustice to flourish in personal and systemic forms.

My reflections here are grouped under those three broad categories. They are presented as a sequence but actually function more like a spiral. I offer a palette of observations to provide color and texture so we might come to perceive, name and act more justly. This is the change in you and in me that the world awaits. This is the new life toward which Christian worship relentlessly urges us to move. Until our worship actually leads us to love differently in the world, our hearts have not changed.

Throughout this book, I use *worship* to mean living the life God made us for—in other words, the most encompassing response of the whole of our lives to the whole of God made known in Jesus Christ. Worship is sharing in the life that is God's life in and for the world. Worship, then, will not refer to a particular form, musical or liturgical. It refers to the life-encompassing act of waking up to God in Christ by the Spirit with our whole being, living in communion with others who are doing likewise, and letting it show in the midst of a world for which such wakeful worship is to be a daily taste of the kingdom of love and justice that is coming.

How should you read this book? The content here will be simple and possibly even familiar to you. But what is not simple is moving from these observations to a transformed heart that looks more like that of Jesus Christ. I invite you to linger. This is not at all a book meant to be run through. In fact, doing so might cause the book to backfire. I am trying to offer sustained reflection on things that are not light or easy. Too much at a time could be discouraging. I am confident that God longs to transform us in the ways I try to describe, but God is seldom instantaneous about doing the most significant things.

I believe it is best to read one chapter for several days before moving to the next, praying that the Holy Spirit will use it to prompt you in the course of those days to focus on how you see, name and act in the world. The questions at the end of each section can be used for individual consideration or for group discussion. Then, at the end of each major section of the book you will find a set of deeply encouraging biblical texts that I invite you to take time to meditate over as a source of inspiration and joy. The work we do here is serious, but as C. S. Lewis says, "Joy is the serious business of Heaven."[2] The goal is not to finish this book, but to seek a transformed heart that is filled with God's joy. If we do so, it will show up in changed lives that do justice as a mirror of the God we worship. That is what makes loving our neighbors dangerous—dangerous to our selfish absorption. I know—I write this book because I must face this danger to gain more of the heart of Jesus.

My hope is that these meditations work their way into your heart and mind. These perspectives and experiences are changing me, and I offer them in the hope that they may do the same for you. May God use them to expose our hearts to the clarifying light of the grace of God; to rename ourselves, our neighbors and God accordingly; to abandon the dismissive ways we distance ourselves from "them" rather than living in God's world of "us"; and, as a consequence, to enact the justice of God in ordinary ways and through daily courage in tangible action. This is the worship God seeks. It reflects the God whose heart sends you and me to be the personal evidence of God's love in a world of suffering. God's glory and people's lives depend on it.

In the simplest terms, what I am saying is that the world would be more just if we had hearts that were more like God's. Of course, to put it that plainly invites believer and skeptic alike toward con-

---

[2]C. S. Lewis, *Letters to Malcolm: Chiefly on Prayer* (San Diego: Harvest, 1964), p. 93.

descension, if not derision: "So, your point is that if we were more like God and less like ourselves, the world would be a better place? Well, there's a fresh and useful idea!" many might say, dismissive of what seems idealistic and unrealistic. Ever ready to be my own harshest skeptic, I understand that response.

A WORK OF FICTION?

One day, nearing the end of writing this book, I was holding the manuscript on my lap while seated on an airplane next to what felt like a nosy neighbor. She saw the title page on top of the loose pages before me and asked in an annoying voice, "What are those papers you are holding? Are you the writer?" I curtly responded. Then, in a rather aggressively elongated way, "Is . . . is . . . is that a work of fiction?" I abruptly grunted "no," but then added, "Well, I suppose that's the real question." Without rejoinder, she suddenly changed seats, while I fell into a meditative trance: is this book a work of fiction?

Is it a work of fiction to talk about changing the human heart in order for the world to become more just? Am I merely fabricating, out of my own theological tradition and personal imagination, a set of observations and admonitions about a make-believe world with less suffering? Am I making up a hope for a more just world—earnest, thoughtful, compassionate, perhaps, but more helpful for Oz than for Oakland?

From the start, followers of Jesus have wondered something similar: is the kingdom of God Jesus' fantasy, or is it a real, if not yet fulfilled, hope? Believing it's the latter, Jesus himself is the greatest evidence of the realism of the kingdom. The Bible bears unique testimony to him, and those who follow Jesus are meant to be ordinary, everyday evidence for the presence of the kingdom's reality. That is how Jesus' followers are to live. In the minds of some, however, this is exactly what begs the question: do those who claim to follow Jesus live showing God's heart for righteousness and justice?

A fictional world can never be lived. If the kingdom that we affirm is not lived, it is easy to understand why people infer that such a kingdom must be fictional. If we say we love God and don't love our neighbor, it turns out we don't love God. In other words, our faith is only fiction.

The heart of God calls us to demonstrate the reality of God's kingdom. Jesus Christ calls his disciples to have hearts that beat to a different vision, that are formed by a different narrative and that courageously seek a different kingdom. What will show the world that this is true is how we actually love and seek justice.

Is this a work of fiction? I know the cynics' response. I know the dogmatic response. Our true response will be how we actually live. It's yours and mine to answer. But what matters even more is that God's answer to whether this is a work of fiction is a resounding no. It is as sure as this:

> When [Jesus] came to Nazareth, where he had been brought up, he went to the synagogue on the sabbath day, as was his custom. He stood up to read, and the scroll of the prophet Isaiah was given to him. He unrolled the scroll and found the place where it was written:
> "The Spirit of the Lord is upon me,
>   because he has anointed me
>   to bring good news to the poor.
> He has sent me to proclaim release to the captives
>   and recovery of sight to the blind,
>   to let the oppressed go free,
>   to proclaim the year of the Lord's favor."
> And he rolled up the scroll, gave it back to the attendant, and sat down. The eyes of all in the synagogue were fixed on him. Then he began to say to them, "Today this scripture has been fulfilled in your hearing." (Lk 4:16-21)

God's yes in Christ makes our yes an act of hope.

Part One

Discovering Where We Live

Our Address

Learning our address takes a lifetime. That's not how I saw it in first grade. Like many other things at that point, my address seemed simple. I remember the deliberateness with which my parents taught me our house number and the name of our street. This had two great benefits as they explained it: (1) I would know where I was, and (2) if I ever got lost, a policeman or another grownup could help me find my way home.

At the time, it seemed like heady stuff. I think it was that same first-grade year I was asked to fill out a form and put this crucial information in the right boxes: 323 53rd Avenue, Yakima, Washington 98902. It felt grownup to be able to name my geographical location.

This became more exhilarating when I realized later on how expansive my full address was: U.S.A., North America, Western Hemisphere, Northern Hemisphere, Earth, Solar System, Cosmos. At seven years old, I was sure I had my address nailed. In fact, however, that was a bit like thinking that because I had made it up the big hill on my walk to school, I now understood mountains. What I thought I had completed, I was only just beginning.

The problem was that my understanding of my address was not yet specific enough. At that stage in my development, I couldn't see the still more defining particularities of my nuclear or extended family—our racial, social, economic, educational, political and spiritual locations that were actually more important to my personal address than our house numbers. All the children I shared classrooms with thought we experienced life in similar ways, but our lives were, in fact, quite different from one another in their particularities. If that was true of fellow students at Roosevelt Elementary, how much more would it be so for children in poorer parts of town, or those who lived on the Yakima Reservation, or who temporarily resided in farm-worker camps outside town. My social location was much more specific than I had understood. When measured in comparison to children a few miles away, let alone to children and adults in other parts of the world, our addresses were farther apart than I had begun to grasp. Like most children, I thought local was global.

I began to understand my address more specifically when I was seventeen and had the chance to go with a friend to Europe by ourselves for five weeks. My parents felt comfortable with this in part because we had distant relatives to stay with for part of the trip. But even more basic was an instinct in my parents that my buddy and I could be trusted to the world, and the world could be trusted to us. That was itself a very important reflection of where we lived in the world. What I learned on this trip was that the rest of the world did not live at my address or even near my neighborhood. And further, I wanted to know much more about what it was like to live at theirs. I had stepped through a door I would never want to close.

On the one hand, we encountered the glory of historical, architectural and artistic achievement that I found captivating. On the other hand, there was the underbelly of life, human greed, power and war that were really discouraging and depressing. It was plainer than I could have expected: life was not a choice between one world and another. The contradictions and tensions seemed to be true whether you were talking about political leaders or artists, ordinary citizens or governments, individuals or societies. The glory and the ugliness, the justice and the injustices, seemed to go together whatever the country, the century or the status of those in view. This was my story and our story. I was beginning to understand that my address was at once both more particular and more universal than I had realized.

This large-scale human drama showed itself in small vignettes on our trip. One of these took place on a nearly empty bus in the beautiful French countryside. As my friend and I were riding along, a kindly looking older man got on the bus and made his way to a seat several rows in front of ours. A couple of stops later, two teenage boys about our age got on and sat behind us on the bus. Bored, they were clearly looking for some way to entertain themselves. The cheerful, slight, older man became their target. First, they aggressively and loudly moved into the empty seat right behind him. Their initial greeting to him seemed to imply a friendly familiarity, but with a sinister attitude. This was a starting point for what quickly became their torment. Their voices mocked him. They flipped off his beret again and again, calling him names, jabbing him with insults and physically picking at him. The man said nothing, but as he slunk down in his seat, his face and neck flushed in a humiliated silence that only added to the mortification he conveyed. When the next stop came, the boys ran off and the rest of us rode on. The man lowered his head, cap off. When my friend and I eventually came to our stop, we got off, but I couldn't leave the bus incident behind me.

I had certainly seen kids fight and badger each other, and especially older boys pick on younger ones. I had seen a cat tyrannized by bullies. But I had never seen an older, weak, timid man be humiliated and harassed by a couple of punks. My friend and I knew only cryptic French. We had made gestures of protest and didn't get the response we anticipated. The scene had lasted for only a few minutes but it haunted me for days. I can still remember how disturbing, even sickening, I found it. It was pointless tyranny. Those minutes felt like such a perversity of our shared humanity, so demeaning to the specific man and to the tormentors as well. I felt shame that we are people who could do that to another human being, for entertainment. It left a sort of searing mark on my heart. It was a deep, intimate sort of injustice that happened simply because it could.

I returned to the States for my senior year of high school, a time full of activity and anticipation. Underneath the busyness, however, I was asking questions about myself and about the world I was seeing. Some of this wrestling had to do with suffering brought on by large political issues like the Vietnam War and the civil rights movement. Some of my questions swirled around the individual and our universal capacity to be bullies. As I thought about my future, I knew I wanted to live in a way that mattered for good (however I understood that at the time). But to what purpose? Guided by what vision?

Those questions and the encouragement of a teacher eventually brought me to the New Testament, and especially the Gospels. On my own, I actually read Matthew, Mark, Luke and John. I was repelled. I was drawn. I was repelled. I was drawn. I was fearful, but I was hopeful. I was unconvinced. I was drawn. I was met. I was convinced. By the end of the following summer, a year after the summer in Europe, with big questions and the draw of college filling me, I grappled my way through the Gospels again and again. I couldn't prove to anyone, including myself, that the gospel was true, but I did come to believe that if it were true, it was more important that I learn to follow Jesus than that I do anything else, that to follow Jesus meant not withdrawing but going further into the lives and circumstances of the world around me. I quietly and sincerely decided to put my trust in Christ (my chief terror being that it would mean I would have to become a pastor, the last thing I would ever have envisioned). What I could see was that to follow Jesus meant living as a servant of God's love.

What was clear to me then was that Jesus came to realign power in the world, to rescue and redeem humanity in order that human beings would thrive in the terms and intentions of our Maker's heart. It was true for the humiliated man on the bus, for the bullying boys. It was true for the people and institutions with the most power, and for those who had little or none. It was true for me.

My heart wanted me for my sake. God's heart wanted me for God's sake. I came to believe that God's heart was more trustworthy in defining and shaping the welfare of my heart than I was. The trustworthiness of God's love was a surprising discovery to me, and was central to why I came to follow as Jesus' disciple. I knew at that point to follow the heart of Jesus was also going to be central to my future, whatever it would mean.

And it has been. I had imagined a future in international relations and politics. What unfolded was a call to pastoral ministry, to preach and teach for the sake of what God wanted to do through his people in a spiritually hungry and unjust world. In other words, my life involved the future I least envisioned, and which has always been such a surprise to me. God led me into a life that engages with the world—but with an unexpected twist.

Now I lived in Christ in the world. That was my new address and it affected everything (Phil 1). It meant the world was bigger and deeper, that things close at hand and far away all mattered more. It meant that my life was no longer my own or simply about me. I was beginning the process of losing my life in order to find it. The newspaper, the ambulance siren, the homeless panhandler, the child in Biafra all began to appear like parts of a new neighborhood, familiar but changed.

When I got my mailing address memorized in first grade, I had no idea that fifty years later I would still be trying to understand my location, with the implications of where I live. Still. I admit that even in Christ I live on this side of things, over here, in a world of middle- and upper-middle-class white assumptions, and that my heart has a long way to go to look and act like the heart of Jesus.

> **Reflection.** *What words capture your social and spiritual location in the world? Which aspects of your social or spiritual location do you think are the most influential in your life? Which aspects do you think most affect others you encounter? Why? What observations do these factors lead you to make?*

IT'S ALL GOOD (OVER HERE)

Where we live shapes how we live. That's our story. If you are reading this, you probably also live on "this side of things." For most who do, the world looks pretty good most days. It's always possible to wish for more, of course. A bigger flat-screen TV. A nicer home. A more stable economy and portfolio. More time would always be good. But really, all things considered, from this side of things, the world doesn't look too bad.

We have to admit that growing up here means that many basic elements of life are readily accessible: food and water, for starters. On this side, food is about what you like and how you like it, when and where you want it. Food is about choices and preferences. Thousands of new grocery products are added to shelves yearly. Meals happen with daily regularity. Some we like more than others. Some are treats and celebrations. Meals can be simple or fancy, everyday or for a special occasion. Some may be at home, some at a relative's or friend's, some at restaurants. But they happen and keep happening, and, frankly, we wouldn't have it any other way.

Water—for drinking, bathing, swimming, playing, showering, irrigating, cooking—is what we turn on without a thought or even a hesitation. We need and want it, so we have it. It will be clean, drinkable, refreshing. From the moment we wake till we take our last sip from the cup at our bedside, water simply is and is ours. We assume that should be so and it will be so. Since water is essential for our life, we would not imagine things otherwise; that's what makes it life on this side.

Electricity is another thing. We hardly think that flipping the light switch and expecting illumination is an audacious hope. Not if we live on this side of things. For babies, turning on a light bulb may be simple entertainment; for the rest of us, doing so is merely incidental to the next task, the next step. We may turn it on and leave it on, with or without energy-saving bulbs. We don't have to think about it. With our unthinking access to electricity comes the chance to turn on the stove, to plug in a power strip, to charge batteries, to start the computer and log into the universe of the Internet. If we have electricity, we've got power, and power in more terms than we can even see.

Shelter is also on the list of good things about this life. The exceptionalism of the homeless population actually underlines the normalcy of having shelter on this side of things. Our homes vary vastly, but whether they're owned or rented, we expect to live under stable cover, with reliable and sealed walls, doors, windows and locks. A place to lay our heads, to feed, clean and set our bodies. To organize our lives as we choose is assumed. Protection from the elements of the physical and social environments we publicly live in. A discrete, recognizable address to which mail or visitors or emergency vehicles could arrive comes with our shelter, even as it identifies and locates us in our social setting. This means that if strong winds or even heavy rains pound where you live tonight, the walls, windows and roof will still be standing in the morning. In fact, you may just sleep through it.

Safety comes as another of our life's baselines. Accidents can happen. Theft and attacks occur, but we carry an assumption of safety that means we wake up to get on with more than self-defense or self-protection. On this side of things, we can eat, play, work, study, worship without fear, with genuine confidence that we are safe to do these things without encountering danger. Should it occur, we have the benefit of reliable and trustworthy emergency medical and police services that would come to help us, and behind that an appeal to the rule of law that serves to embody a commitment to social safety and justice. Whether I can afford it or not, all this is in some measure there for my benefit as part of living on this side of things.

Wrapped into the benefit of all these wonderful things then is the possibility, if not probability, that we don't need to think all that much about them. Of course, the fact is we do think about each of them quite a lot. But we are choosing to do so, not because these things are fundamentally lacking but because we want more of them. The name for the crisis of life on this side of things is *more*.

Life on this side is not about having some; it's almost always about having more. So we want clean water to come into our homes, and, if it can, we would like it to pour into a porcelain sink with nickel fixtures. We want more than bread; we want the best whole-wheat loaf, freshly baked and warm, with local, organic butter melting into it. We are glad to live in 1,500 square feet, but life would really be so much more as we want it if we had an additional 500 square feet (with a hot tub, please—to relieve our stress).

Life on this side of things definitely has real pain and genuine desperation. One can have all things that life on this side brings with it and still find life difficult. The anguish of our minds and hearts can almost erase the simple pleasures and privileges of this life—enough so that it can seem as if they don't really matter, in fact. It turns out a person can have unlimited access to food, water and shelter and still feel that life is miserable.

But when our personal life doesn't suck, the world looks pretty good. That's how life is calibrated if you live on this side of things. If my world is OK, then the world is OK. It's true we still have the wars in Iraq and Afghanistan, but mostly they're just a distant distraction. The economic crisis is real, and many people are actually suffering because of it, even though many more of us mostly feel an air of subdued pleasure and a quiet anxiety all around. The cost of gas fluctuates up and down, so we think more about whether and where to drive, but it doesn't really stop most of us from going when and where we want.

What is most invisible to those who live on this side of things is often far more visible to those who look at the world from the other side of things: the access we have to all these and many other forms of power. We don't think of indoor plumbing or ready food or electricity as expressions of personal and social power, but they are. Without these things, we lose access to much of what we have been able to choose, to prioritize, to express.

We don't spend hours getting water, nor are we stymied in our work. Without chronic diarrhea or malaria, we have the energy to work. We don't usually see all this if we live on this side of things.

Whatever. Life on this side of things assumes that life is not about those problems. Here it's all good.

> **Reflection.** *What things that you experience or assume every day about life are part of life on this side of things? Prioritize the top five things for you. How would you respond if three of these things were indefinitely, even permanently, removed from your life? How would you define life in those circumstances?*

IT'S WHAT IT IS (OVER THERE)

Life on "that side of things" just is. Thinking about it as good or bad isn't really the point if you are on that side. Today holds the same demanding familiarities of yesterday and tomorrow. Life on that side of things is what it is.

For starters, whether in Detroit or Dhaka, food and water are not assumed. The main activities of each day will be given over to securing both. It's a family affair that will involve lots of walking,

waiting, standing, gathering, cutting, carrying, squatting, pound-
ing, grinding, swatting, boiling and, hopefully, cooking. This amid
laughter and play, touching and smiling, but never at the cost of
forgetting what's needed: food and water. You work for less than
two dollars a day despite how bad your malaria might be because
without doing that, your children won't eat that day. Selection,
preference, choice don't figure into the day. Securing what's essential does.

Water comes from a distance and requires strength and commitment. Water does not come to where it's needed; people must
go to where it can be found. Then, the real work begins: getting the
water home. Girls' and women's lives are all about this. The distance, the time, the weight of the burden really can't be calculated,
and must simply be borne. Because water is what water is, there is
only one thing to do. No alternative matters. It may be clean, it
may not, but you have to have it.

Life on that side means that electricity will be spare and unreli-
able. The artificial extension of day into night might happen. It
might be that you have the right wires and fixture, and a working
bulb or outlet. When the switch is flipped, however, you never
know what will occur: nothing, a short-out, a fire, light. Only after you see what happens can you make a plan for the evening's
next step.

Shelter, on that side of life, will hopefully mean at least some
kind of covering above and maybe something like walls. When
there are walls, paint would not hold (even if it were a priority) and
the wallpaper might be newsprint. Doors, windows and locks are
highly discretionary. A typical home will be one room. Any ani-
mals that sleep inside the shelter with you are more likely to be
goats, cows or chickens than cats and dogs.

The safety that exists for life on that side of things has more to
do with relationships than with systems. Exposure's the rule; vulnerability's the norm. It's the absence of power. What safety can be

found lies within the huddle of the family, the tribe, the friend or the tradition. Appeals for help beyond these personal ones would be questionable at best, and possibly even make you susceptible to pressures that could intensify the risk a child or woman might face. Weather, disease, vermin, sanitation, illiteracy—all place lives at risk. Safety is a limited hope held by a thin thread.

For life on that side of things, these are the concerns of every day and every night. These are the worries and fears, the pressures and uncertainties that compel your attention and marshal your day's efforts. Hospitality, joy, love, dreams, laughter, tenderness, wisdom are all things that thrive on that other side of things—as though they have been planted in good soil, sometimes in more verdant abundance than is true for life on this side of things. Here the marginal things make fewer claims on life. So in the midst of all that is not, there can still be love and affection and hope that's free and available. But this is no "happy nativism." Rather, it's resilience and hope.

Then, add to that mix any of the following: drought, war, slavery, being female, failed states, drugs, flooding, being disabled, violence, embargoes, disease, racism, unchecked inflation, the absence of the rule of law, refugee status, forced migration or any of the other common traumas that accompany life on that side of things. The distance between that other side of things and this side of things grows exponentially.

So consequential is this distance, in fact, that it begins to seem like a different reality, another world. The basic factors of everyday life aren't calculated on the same scales. Human nature is held in common, but human experience is breathtakingly distinct.

All this contributes to a lack of power on that side of things. Perhaps there is tremendous personal resilience and capacity. Perhaps there is great creativity, compassion, love and imagination. There may be great vision and potential leadership. But where there is little or no access to appropriate social, economic or legal power, the inhabitants move from circumstances of deprivation toward ones of injustice. Then the address doesn't just indicate poverty but possibly even more virulent, if not violent, oppression.

It turns out that it's not all good on that side of things: life is what it is.

> **Reflection.** *What would be the biggest differences in life if you lived on that other side of things? What if hope meant survival, not improvement or alleviation of daily problems? How would your prayers change?*

IF YOU JUST KEEP MOVING

This side of things.   That side of things.

It's all good.   It's what it is.

For some on this side of things the polarization that exists is just not on the radar. More imminent, personal or pressing things absorb life's energies and thoughts. Our commitment to managing personal security—the dual need to avoid danger, dissonance or distastefulness on the one hand, while pursuing the familiar, the pleasurable and the desirable on the other—takes up a lot of time and effort. Organizing life to this end is no simple task.

To do so requires our attention, money, strategy, planning, priorities. It means work. Forty to eighty hours of work each week, without a lot of say or leeway about what you think about or what gets the best part of your day. That effort will demand doing whatever is required to get the job done. Many of us want and expect it to lead to promotions, gains, bonuses, upward-mobility ladders, a more and more advanced and consuming version of the earlier stages. This is what allows our sense of security to grow. The economics of security define the quality of security, and more rather than less is always preferred.

Doing everything necessary or possible to make life secure is the main goal. Finding, renting and hopefully owning your own home is primary. So too is a good job with medical benefits and the right sort of incentives for gain. Then comes relative proximity to life's other accommodations: food, transportation, recreation—within appropriate distances, at acceptable cost, with desirable variations. Keeping this matrix free, stable and growing is the essence of the American dream.

Let's then imagine adding other significant elements: a spouse, children, a car or cars, investments, bills, insurance claims—all security signifiers. Each takes time, effort, attention and money, and each requires more of it to be secure.

The hope for many of us on this side of things is for signs of our security not to look shabby and, in fact, to look discreet, be subtle, be beautiful or all of the above. It's a new road bike, locked up behind the automatic garage door of a beautiful home with an extensive (but invisible) alarm system, with a small (but visible) security company sign just at the edge of the driveway. To live on this side of things is not accidental. Not simple. Not neutral.

Then when you leave to go somewhere else, you want to travel securely as well. That means a car, and if at all possible, one that is far more than just operational. It means, if possible, having an automotive version of the security and style of the home you have or wish you had. This system also needs to be maintained. The electronic locks, lights, tires, hub locks, keys, alarm systems, all need to be operational. The feel of the seats, the quality of the sound system, the expression of financial and social status represented by the car need to add to the total sense of security you want to maintain when out and about. It may be the sensible story of a Honda Civic, the more ostentatious pronouncement of a full-sized Mercedes, the high suspension of an F-150 pickup or the overreaching aggression of a Hummer.

We on this side of things choose to work out our security differently, of course. It may have to do with education, emotional and social intelligence, street savvy, physical or sexual power. But however it happens, it takes a lot of time, effort and usually money, which means we don't have a lot left over for what seems distant or difficult or undesirable. Besides, we measure our lives against what we don't yet have, because it seems to us that all this stuff is just "normal." What is mostly apparent to us is all we don't have, rather than all we might yet have. "More" is always an attractive option. Still, we are unimpressed with the suggestion that any of this is power.

This does not seem to be a matter of choice. It seems to be the way life is, the way everyone lives, even if some don't. We think of ourselves as usually doing less of all this than we could imagine, and often less than we think we actually should. We can always find people who have so much more than we do that it always seems we are on the middle to low end of this strenuousness cycle.

We can peek out and see and feel for others beyond this side of things, maybe even catching a glimpse of that other side. But we are like rubberneckers on the freeway—maybe we look, but then the momentum picks back up and we get on with where we were headed. We may not even remember we ever slowed down or saw anything that should keep us from the mall. And rubberneckers never help. They just slow things down and annoy everyone. The pressure is on: just keep moving.

Reflection. How does your life's momentum affect your capacity for empathy: entering into the lives and needs of others, especially those who have no tie or evident benefit to your life? Notice today or this week the time and energy you devote to engage with the needs of others. What does empathy cost you? How do you feel about that price?

Paying Attention
to Paying Attention

The word *we* names our sightlines. *We* refers to the boundaries of a way of seeing. It's true, each of us can only live life in the first person. But *we* is not neutral. *We* share with some others a lens that may be built into every frame of reference. Experience, categories, personality, gender, language, race, culture combine to form why and how we see. We are inevitable perspectivists. That is, by the nature of our limitations, we can see only from a limited angle and within a limited range. No human being or society escapes this boundary, even though we may frequently claim to do so.

Our vision is not only a limited frame; it's biased. *We* is life seen from the perch of our own self-interest. Our sightlines are by no means neutral or comprehensive. They are simply what and how we see. That is why what we see appears to us to be so obvious, so unfiltered. Our perception is that we are simply seeing what is.

THE "WE"

We is a set of invisible goggles we never take off, not least because we have no sense we even have them on. We look out on the world with the lenses of our instincts and social grooming. We think we see the way others do, or even more frequently perhaps the reverse: that others see the way we do. In fact, the process is more variable and subtle than that, because the distortions of our lenses are not readily apparent, certainly not to us. We may see similarly to those who share our life lenses, which means we may not see the world that many others see.

Of course, daily social and political life makes it abundantly clear that we don't all see alike. We can see only relatively. But internally, in our hearts, we commonly assume that what we see is the way things are, and that others, if they were seeing accurately, would see things the way we do. They are obviously seeing in filtered, if not distorted, ways. When we are with people we feel we have the most in common with, with whom we may be the least guarded, we find that this has in part to do with many values and assumptions that we hold so much in common because that's what it means to feel at home. We are clear about how we see.

We is more than just a series of shared observations. It is more like a finely tuned set of alarms that neurologically registers fear and monitors safety. Body language, smell and eye movement, skin color, style of dress, volume of voice, attitude and so much more end up telling us from very early on whether we feel we are fundamentally safe or not. *We* can mark out our safety zone and define a terrain in which we feel at home and protected. That terrain may be emotional, social, physical, cultural or political. We go to the gym we do because it has our kind of people. We go to the restaurants or clubs we do because it's our crowd. We shop where we do because those stores "get" us.

When we feel some kind of "threat response," our unease might register to others as prejudice, awkwardness, inexperience, lack of confidence or something else. Internally, it may feel like an instinctive warning system that leads us to look for corroborating details of *otherness*—general personal appearance, clothing, accent, physical proximity, facial expression, eyes, cleanliness, speech or whatever—which lead us to conclude that *we* are seeing *them*.

As *we* see them, we are usually blind to the influence of how profoundly the goggles we are wearing constitute our perception. Crosscultural experiences may be ones we seek or avoid in part because of the comfort or discomfort *we* may have with that "other." We can be highly sophisticated in reading our own culture's cues, knowing just what a certain style or phrase or gesture might subtly convey. But that refined capacity can be worth little or nothing when *we* encounter dimensions of life among people who live in a significantly different culture. We literally don't know what we are seeing or how they are seeing.

This might be an invitation into discovering such meaning. If we accept the invitation, we can learn with some measure of openness and hope. But *we* typically don't give them such opportunity or entrée. Instead, they are just placed in a box labeled "they." We place *them* where *we* think they belong. And *we* move on.

Reflection. Who are in your concentric circles of "we"? What typical signals tell you that someone is part of "your people"? What tells you they are not "your people"? Why? What makes someone or others "they"? What observations can you make of these distinctions? What do they tell you about your heart? Are you close to any or many you consider "they"?

IT'S PLAIN AS FACT

We live on this side of things.   They live on that side.

We as a word opens our mouths, maybe even with smiles. It's an expression of welcome, of ease, of receptivity. It feels familiar to say, and it names the familiar we know. It is a word spoken by inhaling, drawing in the air *we* want and need. It's a basic word. It's a word that gathers in an identity while it also asserts one.

What follows from the enunciation of *we* is an expression of feeling or action that includes me and grounds me in some kind of collective being or performance. We are right . . . we are together . . . we are going out . . . we are eating dinner . . . we are like this . . . we do this.

Saying *we* is like building a kind of perch for ourselves. *We* functions, then, as a kind of social place from which we see, act, engage or withdraw from them and that. It's a powerful perch that motivates so much about how we perceive, name and understand ourselves in the world.

On this side of things, *I* forms the basic building block of *we*. The way the story works on this side of things is that it takes *I* or *me* to make *we*. In a lot of American society, the assumption is that *I* is the core and *we* is the product produced by the free choices that lead us into common, shared associations. We should never expect of *I* anything more than *I* wants to give.

I yields to *we* variably, on this side of things. *We* is typically valued so long as it is either inescapable or useful: family, ethnicity, privilege, opportunity, belonging, love, hope, money. When *we* becomes a significant disappointment or distraction or diversion from what *I* want, or if *we* becomes a force that feels threatening to *I*, then the loyalty to *we* wanes; things change. Easily, readily, a slide occurs: *we* becomes *they*. This is a localized version within life on this side of things that happens in a broader version when applied to the *they* who live on that side of things.

They as a word involves figuratively sticking out our tongue. It's a word of expulsion. *They* is a word that pushes away. It's not far from spitting. It draws a boundary, a perimeter, a distinction, a separation, a distance. *They* is a kind of anti-identity, an anti-definition of *I* or *we*.

They means disassociating, disconnecting: they are like this . . . they think this . . . they feel that . . . they are different because . . . they don't get it the way we do.

Reflection. What moments or circumstances expose your distance, fear, rejection, anger, prejudice, dislike of "they"? Why do these responses seem natural and justified? What experiences or voices in your life have contributed to that?

NOT A PROBLEM

To the words "Thank you very much," the expected response has always been, "You're welcome." This used to be the mannerly pattern. But that seems to be changing.

With increasing frequency, the "response du jour" has become "Not a problem."

How did we move from "You're welcome" to "Not a problem" and not notice that we *have* a problem? Do the assumptions in this new rejoinder expose a significant shift in our relationships with one another? This is not only a matter of manners. To say "You're welcome" carries with it an acknowledgment of the dignity of the person who thanked you, your intentionality as the giver and even the value of the gift. Those small words, whether spoken thoughtfully or reflexively, acknowledge our efforts on behalf of another, an exchange of hospitality or of service. "Thank you" and "You're welcome" can be spoken when being served a cup of tea, interviewed for a job, ushered to a seat or shown the plot of your father's grave. "Thank you very much" is as appropriate to say to someone who threw his or her body in front of the bus to save you as it is to a person who brought you ketchup for your fries. That phrase is serviceable, flexible and respectful—as is the reply "You're welcome."

"Not a problem" puts us in an entirely different relational terrain. That phrase assumes that the service offered is primarily measured by the cost to the one serving. When I ask again for the Diet Coke I had ordered and the server brings it to the table, I say, "Thank you." When the server responds with "Not a problem" (or its variant, "No problem"), something significant has been lost and changed. The server's reply seems to indicate that the value of this exchange is measured by not inconveniencing the person who is there to serve. No-cost service. Service without a problem, hassle, complication— to the server. I see this as a suggestive cultural shift.

The fact is, however, that a lot of the service we need to receive and to offer in our world is really going to be a problem. And that is not itself the primary problem. To step in and serve in any true act of love will involve us in problems, even if it doesn't always mean dealing with the tread marks from the bus. In daily relationships with family, friends and colleagues we step into real and messy experiences. Our lives are meant to carry and share in the problems of others. And that's "not a problem"; that's called love. It's the reason we exist, and it's meant to be the way we spend our lives. Our goal is not to keep the cost of love as low as possible.

Or is it? Those of us on this side of things need to admit that part of what influences our lives is that we just don't want to be a problem. We don't want the label of being told we are one. We want to avoid being the cause of eye-rolling or hand-wringing. So "not a problem," when said to us, is a statement of our success. It's like a cultural blessing: "You didn't irritate me, inconvenience me, degrade or demean me by asking me to bring you the Diet Coke, which I am being paid to do. It's not a problem." Phew!

We don't want their service to have been a problem to them because, in our social economics, this means that their service does not cost us. It's just the price of the Diet Coke. It doesn't require more than that we pay the bill and add an appropriate tip to reward the person for doing their job. What's not a problem for them is not a problem for us. That's just the nonobligating, sacrifice-free zone we like.

Then we hear Jesus' call to love not only those who love us but also those who may be our enemies—and that is exactly what we are supposed to do. That is the real problem, the deeply problematic life of love that is meant to be our daily work. That was what Doris did. That's what I often don't do.

Jesus came down from giving his Sermon on the Mount, in which he revealed the pure, sacrificial heart of God, and immediately encountered a leper (Mt 8). In order to keep all others sacramentally clean, lepers had to announce as they walked down the street, "Unclean! Unclean!" so others would stay away. It was a lot worse than walking down the street shouting, "I'm a problem! I'm a problem!" Still, on this occasion a leper said to Jesus, "If you choose, you can make me clean." Jesus (Matthew tells us) replied, "I do choose. Be made clean!" And Jesus touched him. That turned out to be part of the bigger problem, which Jesus relentlessly accepted: the problem of laying down his life for others. As I see it, however, if people on this side of things are willing to do that at all, it's usually for other people on this side of things, not over on that side. Our hearts don't usually stretch that far.

No wonder we are drifting toward "not a problem" as a cultural maxim. In a vast, needy and messy world, we don't really want to give or receive something that would be a problem, especially for life on this side of things. We are very anxious about being overwhelmed. We fear it, in fact. By contrast, Jesus said that following him would mean living in a way that would be a problem for us, as it was for him. It's called taking up our cross (Mt 16).

Reflection. Do you invest energy daily in avoiding problems or pain—in your life and in the lives of those you love? in the lives of those you work with? What does this lead you to see in your heart? Who is someone you know who does a good job of stepping toward the needs of others? Why do you think so?

WHAT'S INSIDE IS OUTSIDE

We all have heart problems. It's not just the story of what goes on inside us, but of how we act in the world. That condition is not just an inward fact but also an outward reality. Our heart scan is revealed in the details of our daily lives.

The God revealed in Jesus Christ takes the inward and the outward seriously. To be conformed to the likeness of Jesus requires change in both directions. This leads me to affirm that these two are inseparably intertwined both in their current condition and in the process of their transformation:

- To act justly in public is to share and participate in the heart of God (Is 58; Lk 10:25-37).

- To share in God's just and merciful heart means acting that out in public (Mt 5–8; Lk 4:14-41).

For either and both of these dimensions to be lived with some consistency and joy, merely conforming to external laws or assuming an earnest pretense that masks self-interest won't cut it. Neither will talking about an unachievable inward and outward vocation that leads us into the dead end of a perfectionist's paralysis.

What starts in our hearts makes its way onto our lips; what we misperceive, we then misname. The taxonomy of our heart's brokenness produces stereotypes, labels, epithets, curses, categories, hierarchies, and inner and outer rings, all of which frame us, our neighbors and God with a taxonomy of injustice. Out of the heart comes the language that gives and also takes life.

It's ultimately not words that name people, but people—people with misperceiving hearts. And too often the donkey in our hearts gets the last word.

Such a fundamental need in our human condition has never been adequately addressed by reform efforts, education, political or social theory. The crisis is more acute and intractable than human effort can alter. This is part of why the Bible says we need a Savior, someone who can do for us what we need in our core and cannot do for ourselves.

The way out of the crisis is not a religion, a spiritual law or a theological pathway. It's not crassly interposing Christian filters into our hearts and putting Christian language onto our lips. What Scripture invites us to do instead is to dwell, that is, "abide," in a different place, in the heart of God. We are called to find this new life by a daily practice of dying to ourself and being raised for life in Christ, whose life, death and resurrection make this possible. This is how we live out what we and our world most need: a new heart. It's our new address in the midst of the old ones. This language is familiar to many Christians but seems vague and unpracticed. We are to practice seeking justice because it is the heart of God, not because of a system or institution or ideology.

When Jesus says that what we need to do is obey the first and second commandments, he is telling us what we were made to do but cannot, as well as what we must and will do if we are to enter into his life: The first commandment is that "'you shall love the Lord your God with all your heart, and with all your soul, and with all your mind, and with all your strength.' The second is this, 'You shall love your neighbor as yourself'" (Mk 12:30-31).

To do this requires a heart change. If we enter into the heart of Jesus Christ who truly sees and rightly names—himself, his neighbor and God—and leads us to do likewise, we will share in the life that is God's life in the world. The gospel of the kingdom is what comes from the heart of God. That is what our Lord longs to have come from our hearts as well. A lifestyle of worship grounded in the One who is love and justice is our only hope for truly seeing, naming and acting justly in the world.

Reflection. Write a letter to God about your heart in relation to your life in a world of suffering and injustice. Try to explain to God the current state of your heart and the changes you think would be needed to make your heart like God's. Do you desire this change? How will you pray for it? Who in your life could help encourage you in this change? How could you ask them to help?

Sabbath Encouragement

It's time for some sabbath keeping, for rest from the work of self-awareness and critique we have been doing. At the end of this first major section of the book, as we will do at the end of each of the other sections, we are going to take time for some deep breaths before moving on to the next chapters. Looking in the mirror of our own culture or of our own assumptions is not particularly natural or easy. You may dislike it or even reject it. But before going on, it's worth taking some time to pause and remember one of the most foundational and encouraging texts in the whole New Testament:

> If then there is any encouragement in Christ, any consolation from love, any sharing in the Spirit, any compassion and sympathy, make my joy complete: be of the same mind, having the same love, being in full accord and of one mind. Do nothing from selfish ambition or conceit, but in humility regard others as better than yourselves. Let each of you look not to your own interests, but to the interests of others. Let the same mind be in you that was in Christ Jesus,
> who, though he was in the form of God,
>   did not regard equality with God
>   as something to be exploited,
> but emptied himself,
>   taking the form of a slave,
>   being born in human likeness.
> And being found in human form,
>   he humbled himself
>   and became obedient to the point of death—
>   even death on a cross.
>
> Therefore God also highly exalted him
>   and gave him the name
>   that is above every name,
> so that at the name of Jesus

> every knee should bend,
> in heaven and on earth and under the earth,
> and every tongue should confess
> that Jesus Christ is Lord,
> to the glory of God the Father. (Phil 2:1-11)

1. I encourage you to memorize this text, if you have not already done so, and to meditate on it daily.

2. I encourage you to draw great strength and courage from the fact that the self-emptying we seek to do was at the core of Jesus' own sacrifice as well.

3. I encourage you to take hope that though imitating Christ in this way may be difficult, it is central to our call and to what brings exaltation and glory to God.

4. I encourage you to remember as we go on that self-offering love will mean sacrifice, but sacrifice does not finally mean loss but gain, just as it did for Jesus himself.

Take some time to allow part one to continue to steep in your heart. Breath, watch, repent, reflect, receive the good news that God is leading this journey toward a changed heart.

PRAYER

Most gracious God and Father, you are with me as I make my journey throughout this day. Help me to look lovingly upon all people and events that come into my life today and to walk gently upon this land. Grant this through Jesus who lives and walks among us ever present at each moment.

PHYLLIS TICKLE, *THE DIVINE OF HOURS*

Part Two

Seeing

The Problem of Misperceiving

M*itali's story.* For Mitali, the P.E. class started badly and got worse. Growing up as an immigrant in a professional Bengali Hindu family established a baseline for many of the issues in her life. From the high academic expectations of her parents to her status as a third daughter in a sonless South Asian family, along with the usual developmental challenges of growing up, Mitali had plenty of pressure points within her own home.

Her family's move from Queens, New York, to Pleasant Hill, California, only added to this. For one thing, it meant leaving a multihued, multinational neighborhood to settle into a kind of Whiteville in a West Coast suburb. As the only student in her school born outside the United States, Mitali's darker skin underlined the distinction. On top of all this, she was a bright reader and a very shy girl. Mitali was not an athlete.

Various forces predictably converged one day in her new school. Mitali found herself, again, the unchosen one when P.E. teams were picked. Standing alone, unvalued, Mitali heard the boy captain relent in resignation and say, as if to no one, "Fine, then, I'll take that ugly, black thing."

Crushed, cursed, Mitali felt there was really no one to whom she could turn. Her family had its own prejudices and anxieties about skin color stemming from their culture of origin. Whether by family or foe, Mitali was misperceived, and that shaped her every day.

The layering of misperceptions in Mitali's story is part of what makes it illustrative of the problem. At the core, it is about otherness. Layers of performance, conformity, appearance and social benefit get heaped on in such a way that they obscure the actual person. This happens on an individual-by-individual basis, but also in social, racial, economic and educational groups. Fear of otherness is the problem, and, at least often, dominance over that otherness is the means of maintaining equilibrium and assurance, overcoming that fear. That phenomenon is painful. It's destructive. It's everywhere.

Susan's story. Fifteen minutes of fame washed over Susan Boyle after her appearance on *Britain's Got Talent*. When they saw that plain, gray-haired, solid-bodied, Scottish country woman, the judges and people in the audience audibly scoffed when she said she hoped to become another Elaine Paige. Unimaginable. Then she sang. The audience, aghast with surprise, rose in tears to applaud her. An overnight Internet sensation, Susan Boyle got far more than just her original fifteen minutes. Global media attention focused on the astonishing revelation that someone who seemed such a paragon of the ordinary could have such extraordinary talent. She shattered those expectations.

Was the acclaim any more valid an understanding of Susan Boyle than the dismissiveness had been? Recognizing Susan's talent was surely better than not seeing it, but the basic lens of misperception was still as distorted as it had been before the moment of her audition. Now there was talent, performance. Susan Boyle seen dismissively as an ordinary woman with a wonderful voice is only a slightly more informed superficiality than her being seen simply as an ordinary woman. We honor otherness when we enjoy the benefit, but the rules remain the same.

David's story. A slight young boy from a Nairobi slum, David happened to be at the wrong place at the wrong time. The consequences nearly killed him. David ran through an area of police action just as a skirmish was going on over a violent theft. Since that crime is a capital offense in Kenya, and since the culprits slipped away, David became convenient prey for the police to harass, attack and imprison in order to demonstrate their power. They could do what they wished. David could do nothing. In the end, the police fired a gun at David, hitting his wrist and hand. He survived; his hand did not. Then David was thrown in prison, indefinitely, by those whose hearts said of David, "vulnerable and dispensable." As a consequence, David was randomly changed forever.

Elisabeth's story. When Elisabeth, as a young teenager, was sold by her aunt into slavery in a brothel in Southeast Asia, it was in part an act of the heart. It's true that people in desperate circumstances do desperate things and rationalize each step along the way. It's also true that these actions emerge out of the distortions of the heart. The economic poverty of Elisabeth's aunt may have trumped family loyalty, but the trigger was not just the possibility of selling Elisabeth without impunity. It's that her aunt no longer saw her niece for who she really was; it revealed the poverty of her aunt's heart in its desperation and disintegration. Out of the heart of Elisabeth's aunt came an entirely different perception that reduced this lovely young girl, her own sister's daughter, to a commodity. Her aunt's misperception stripped Elisabeth of dignity, hope and innocence. The aunt no longer saw her as deserving the simple joys of adolescence spent in the loving safety of her parents' home. To her aunt, Elisabeth became merely a means.

I have never sold someone nor been sold. Nor have you. I don't think I have it in me to do either, though, in fact, I might be wrong. What we do carry in common is a capacity for radical misperception that involves unjustly and cruelly diminishing others whom God sees as "fearfully and wonderfully made." We usually do so for our sake.

HOW MISPERCEPTION SHAPES SELF-PERCEPTION

Misperception is one of our global, multigenerational nightmares. We invisibly inherit and pass along those triggers of prejudice, hatred, disgust, trivialization that come out of the hearts of our parents, family and friends. What we receive, we pass on. We come to see as those around us have seen. This can be both very good and very bad news. Racism, for example, doesn't spring forth ex nihilo. It comes out of a heart that has been infected by the racist heart of another. Studies of infants show very early signs of registering racial difference based simply on color contrasts. Affinity grouping seems to be a natural instinct when we are born, but the values and attitudes our parents attach to those we see as like or unlike us have a significant effect on how we see and respond to racial differences. Racial prejudice is a universal because it only takes a subhuman heart to treat someone else subhumanly for that to be the norm. History, past and present, tells us we have this proclivity in us.

For one human being to enslave another, for example, requires many layers of misperception, both of and by the slave owner, the slave and the surrounding society. The slave owners have somehow come to see themselves in terms that make the ownership of another person appropriate, desirable or tolerable. It may be driven by a profit motive in which the slave is perceived as a means to an end, or as an animate machine in their delivery system of a product to market (like bricks, rice or bidi cigarettes). The lies about slaves are, of course, closely linked to the slave owners' misperceptions of themselves as well. Slave owners see their self-interest, power and cleverness as appropriately justifying their enslavement of another person. Their capacity to do this and get away with it for enormous profit is all the ground they need to stand on.

Amid the moral distortions of these misperceptions, the slave owners can thrive. As long as they escape consequences, and as long as the profit outweighs the cost, as long as there is social, legal or political blindness that turns away from the real horrors of enslaving others, then slave owners can pragmatically, if not smugly, justify their buying and selling other human beings. By extension, this means that the tens of thousands of slave owners around the world perceive the good, profitable and socially tenable in radically distorted ways. It may be as simple as perceiving the vulnerable as prey. Money is the heart of what matters.

The customers are likewise engaged in distorted perceptions that turn persons into pieces of erotic, disposable flesh. To perpetuate the misperception of selling young virgins, hymens may be repeatedly sewn shut in order for the pain and bleeding to sustain the customer's illusion of getting his fantasy encounter. Because sex trafficking thrives on misperception, billions of dollars are made annually on perpetuating those misperceptions. The story is the same. The names being changed doesn't protect the innocent.

Misperceptions like these are not just mistaken, they are fatal. People made in the image of God—intended to bring honor to the God of the universe, to give and receive love from others who bear that image, to have the capacity to think, dream, imagine, sing, hope—are not rightly valued. Degrees of misperception vary, but far more often than we imagine, human life itself is jeopardized, if not extinguished, by our mis-seeing, both for the victim and the victimizer. And that's not all—we don't need to be in the slave trade to have hearts that readily allow us to treat others as merely a means. We may just be choosing a teammate in a P.E. class. Rationalizing, we let ourselves off the hook with our frames of misperception and words that misname. This then contributes to the social complicity that tolerates Elisabeth's aunt doing what we say is unthinkable, even when it happens all the time.

Reflection. Consider in these next days all the varied ways you perceive the people in the world around you, near and far. What lenses are you using? Why? How do they affect others and what you see about them? When and where do you see those around you, or in other places in the world, as merely a means? Why do you do so? If the tragic headline referred to your sibling or close friend, how differently would you respond?

INJUSTICE ROLLS DOWN

By the time we read reports about injustices near and far, we have heard stories a long way down the road from their beginnings. Before a single tale of bonded slavery or human trafficking has occurred, a long string of factors has enabled the distortion of human relationships to make such horrific things imaginable and doable, maybe even normal and expected. Before a hate crime is committed, a heart has gone tragically wrong and made a world of pain and distortion. Before we emit another sigh of disengagement from a newspaper headline about poverty or AIDS, our hearts tell us that it is not our concern. The sheer ubiquity of this fact makes it both obvious to state and essential to admit. Its obviousness contributes to its invisibility. If "the only thing necessary for evil to prevail is for good [people] to do nothing" (Edmund Burke), what better way of doing nothing than to live in our invisibly socialized deception that injustice is their problem, not ours. It's about those people, not my people; it's about what's *there*, not what's *here*. It's what it is. It's how we casually and daily partition reality.

These baseline presuppositions explain how we can listen but not hear the cries of the suffering. We can be aware of the sexual abuse of someone we read about in our local paper, the violence of our city's gangs, the hunger among the local working poor, and then forget all about it. We can watch a documentary on hunger and then go out to dinner without a pause. We can wish things were better for them, but then get on with our day. We can hope that solutions can be found, circumstances improved, wrongs righted. But it all seems to lie beyond us. Meanwhile, we receive the circumstantial and accidental benefits of "social Darwinism," glad that we are among those surviving, if not thriving. This simultaneously allows us to live with a clear conscience, believing that we are not the perpetrators of injustice while also being convinced that injustice is beyond our power to change. We think this is just the way things are. Most of us find this a tolerable stalemate most of the time. That is true for most of us on this side of things.

The consistent witness of Scripture is that each of us is, in all times and places, implicated, deeply implicated, in the problem of injustice. That problem turns out to be not only there but here, not only about them but as much (and sometimes more) about us. Jesus said, "For out of the heart come evil intentions, murder, adultery, fornication, theft, false witness, slander" (Mt 15:19). This suggestive list from "out of the heart" leaves the door of injustice wide open. What shows up in public is a revelation of what is first in our hearts. This makes Cornel West's observation all the more compelling: "Justice is what love looks like in public" (from the film *Call+Response*). Turning it around, injustice is what shows up when love is absent from the heart.

To admit this, to face it in ourselves, is to tamper with the paradigm, and that is often just too threatening. We may immediately leap to self-defense or self-justification, to blame or rationalization. We want to live in some kind of internal equilibrium about this so as to avoid being overwhelmed or carrying false guilt or becoming paralyzed. These are understandable reactions, part of the apparently neutral and justifiable experience we have when we live on this side of things. Beneath all this is the foundational truth that we don't really love God or our neighbors. Injustice is one of the consequences of our failure of heart. Out of our core comes a profoundly shaping sequence of distortions: misperception, misnaming and misacting in the world. This sequence is replayed over and over again. It's what we think is simply true of life in an unjust world in which many of us generally consider ourselves to be without complicity, responsibility or power. God's heart passionately desires justice, starting with the most vulnerable. Our heart typically does not. The Lord speaks through Isaiah:

> Is not this the fast that I choose:
>> to loose the bonds of injustice,
>> to undo the thongs of the yoke,
> to let the oppressed go free,
>> and to break every yoke?
> Is it not to share your bread with the hungry,
>> and bring the homeless poor into your house;
> when you see the naked, to cover them,
>> and not to hide yourself from your own kin?
> Then your light shall break forth like the dawn,
>> and your healing shall spring up quickly;
> your vindicator shall go before you,
>> the glory of the LORD shall be your rear guard.
> Then you shall call, and the LORD will answer;
>> you shall cry for help, and he will say, Here I am. (Is 58:6-9)

Reflection. *If justice means "to make things right," what is one area of injustice that especially matters to you (or, alternatively, one that you think should matter to you but doesn't yet? Write down ten to fifteen things you could do in the next couple of months to enlarge your understanding and empathy for people in that circumstance. What do you think God's heart feels in response to them? What about yours?*

4 | Learning to See

A man and a woman were standing next to me at the street crossing, intensely arguing with one another, their voices full of disdain and anger. Meanwhile, about ten or more feet away, standing by himself, a three-year-old was screaming plaintively into the air, "I am over here." The parents didn't look at or even acknowledge their child, nor were they looking at each other. The child's sense of invisibility got only more desperate. The parents were lost in their anger toward each other and, at least at that moment, their child was lost to them. This family drama had the appearance of a cycle familiar to each of them. Invisibly, something was being etched in that moment on that child's heart that will show up again and again as his life unfolds.

THE BROKEN IMAGE

Even the most adoring parents imperfectly reflect who we are. The joys, fears and hurts that have shaped them are borne in their faces and are invisibly etched in their children's hearts. So too are the lines of their location, economic situation, racial and ethnic heritage. Good parenting helps us see ourselves more truly, fully and lovingly. At their best, however, our parents nurture us in the only way they can: partially and brokenly. The image they reflect is an incomplete one, with pieces of their broken mirror at varying depths and angles, some parts missing, bearing light at times and hiding it at others. Since they see us as well as fail to see us, what they reflect is inadequate, even when their care is attentive and loving. These effects are in everyone's life, no matter what the privilege or problems that surround us. Privilege can be as profound as deprivation when it comes to our failure to see ourselves. Our circumstance, however varied, show up in our self-perception.

Every family background leaves at best a filtered image of who we are and who we are not, both in ourselves and in relation to our world. As our childhood world expands and we see ourselves through the eyes of many others, this same pattern is reproduced again and again with varying force and effect. We are told by facial expression and gesture, word and sign, who we are and who our neighbors are. Siblings, relatives, friends, teachers, babysitters, principals add to the reflections. Sometimes they get it right, and sometimes they don't. We may not be able to tell the difference that well. We internalize the messages without adequate tools to distinguish the lies from all the rest. In our teenage years the reflection we see of ourselves in the eyes of others can sear our hearts. We become developmentally aware that we are no longer at "home." We have entered a world where we are highly sensitive to others' cues, vulnerable to every nuance of someone else's projected definition of us. Our cognitive, emotional, physical, sexual and social selves are changing and are self-consciously exposed. In middle school, for example, even a new haircut can seem definitional.

This is human social development, whatever the culture or period. What it's not is neutral, let alone reliable or just. Our social location, with all its particularities and defects, substantially affects our way of seeing. If we are raised in a tight ethnic community, for example, the differences between *us* and *them* often form lines in our hearts. The ways we have been seen teach us how to see. We pass on both the clarity and distortion that have been passed on to us. The reflection of our shattered mirror is also cast onto the lives of others. As human beings, we are inescapably meaning-makers, and we grow up and mature in an intricate process of engagement, reflection, encounter, testing and trying to see and know ourselves and one another. Our objective and subjective visions of ourselves and of others comes as one largely inseparable jumble. We practice this at close range with family, with a gradually enlarging group of friends, within the sociology into which we are cast and amid the stimuli that we absorb.

Reflection. What mirrors have you most trusted to show you your image? In what ways have these mirrors told the truth? told lies? How do they affect the capacity you have to see yourself and to see others?

SEEING AS WE ARE SEEN

We look at our reflection all of our lives. What we don't see is that the mirrors we use are distorted. Misperception starts with our self-reflection. We even, if not especially, see ourselves through a glass darkly. How could it be otherwise?

A phone call came just now from a couple who have longed for a baby for several years with repeated anguish, sorrow, needles, hopes, prayers, treatments, loss. Soul-scorching pain. Today's call put an abrupt (and hopefully long-term) end to their slide into discouragement, if not despairing doubt. "We are pregnant" was the simple news. The thin thread by which their hope hung even yesterday became today a modest cord. When, by God's grace, that baby is eventually born, there is not a chance that he or she will ever be seen by these parents in a neutral way. Nor should they see their child neutrally. This will be the most anticipated, longed-for fulfillment in either of their lives. The anticipation that will build in the months to come means that child will be born into a universe of highly reflective relationships. As this baby eventually peers out through his or her two tiny windows into the surrounding world, what will be reflected back will be electrified attention, devotion, delight and hope. All this will be the earliest mirrored reflections that will show and tell this baby who she or he is and that the world is as it should be.

At best, those reflections will be at least partly true. Mom's love will be mixed with mom's insecurity; dad's too. Her delight will also carry her need. Her fears will be conveyed in her expressions; the baby will read her face and gestures, and from them will begin to interpret or infer what is happening and why. The baby will see, but through a glass darkly. This particular baby will eventually be passed around at family gatherings where grandparents, siblings, aunts and uncles are present. This family system, like most, has lots of complexity, competing and colliding visions and hopes. The mirror into which this child will look is broken. Relationships are not all they could be. Disappointment and anger are real, not least toward God. This family, as every family, reflects not just its joys into that baby's tiny windows, but the broken image of themselves and of the baby as well.

I remember the absorbing wonder at our two boys, Peter and Sam, as babies. Although no child comes close to being a blank slate, thankfully, the extraordinary gift of a child is utter openness and vulnerability. Each of our boys even at birth was already and truly himself in some fundamental ways. Their temperament, bodies and personalities were distinctly their own from the start. Yet as infants and toddlers they were also changing in response to the love that my wife, Janet, and I, as loving parents, were giving them and the influence we were having on them. Causal links from parent to child are harder to manage than correlative ones, but either way, for better and worse, our Peter and Sam grew up reflecting parts of us, their parents.

And this is only the start. The baby's tiny twin windows will receive ever-increasing information of greater diversity and sweep from their ever-enlarging world. Life will not be neutral toward them, nor will they be neutral toward the world. The mirrors of others will reflect into their mind, heart and soul all kinds of information that will tell them a jumble of truths and lies about themselves and about each other. So there is no chance that this baby will grow up to see neutrally. The sweet, longed-for baby will become that unmistakable reality we all are: prejudiced seers in a world of competing and confusing diversity who can see only as we are formed to do so, the only way we can. If doting distorts our self-understanding in certain directions, the far more common experience is a narcissistic wound: a profound, internalized sense of deficit arises in our hearts and minds out of the inadequacy of love we receive in infancy and early childhood, or out of the dramas of neglect and abuse. We carry this every day. We see the world through this wound. When you add to this psychological condition the further complications of poverty, disease, hunger, oppression and violence, it can come close to eliminating a person's capacity to see him- or herself, or others, with clarity. Seeing through a glass darkly can be illusive.

> **Reflection.** *Make a list of how you think some of the most important people in your life see you. What do most people who think they see you truly manage to get wrong or fail to see? Why? How influential for you are the views these people hold of you? How do their opinions affect your life? How do their opinions of you in turn affect how you see others?*

SEEING IN ORDINARY

Our eyes: two windows on the world. Not two enormous towers

in the center of the world's commerce, but just tiny windows on the world at the center of nothing but the everyday of our ordinary lives. All the visual information we receive comes through windows on our face less than two square inches in size. We depend on the precision of still smaller lenses and their refractions, their capacity to focus and adjust, as we walk, run, drive or fly through our lives. At sixty-five mph or more, we can recognize a face, read a sign, appreciate various species of wildflowers. As our brain receives, sorts and analyzes this vast database, so these windows allow a constant stream of information to pour in. From our earliest days, we rely on the flood of information that comes to us through our eyes. The bold and the nuanced, the obvious and the subtle, present us with stimuli that our eyes receive and send as signals to no less than twenty-four parts of the brain. Our brain processes this information and has the nearly instantaneous capacity to sort and organize, to read warnings and threats, to recognize and stimulate us to a remarkable range of responses. "We see." It seems so plain, so obvious. Yet often seeing isn't plain or obvious.

Seeing is important and reliable in many ways, but it is neither neutral nor comprehensive. Sight is not just what we see but how we see—and that is a function of values, experiences, relationships, associations, beliefs, culture, race, gender and age. This means that everything we see passes through invisible lenses of perception that take a lot of the information the eye receives and the brain sorts, and place it within the framework of our experience or understanding or plausibility. All this happens in a flash, as a friend wrote about this random moment and encounter:

> I drive 17 miles across a bridge to worship and listen to the words of my favorite pastor of all time. I take notes. This time Matthew 20.1-34. I leave church. It's raining. Umbrella up. I walk up Telegraph. Take a right on Bancroft toward Strada's. A man ap-

proaches in an L. L. Bean hooded-type green jacket. We are about to pass. He steps a little aside from my umbrella. Looks and says, "Rich bitch." I say, "Go to hell." We keep walking.

Spoken or unspoken, our sight filters instantly allow some information in and keep some out, categorizing, framing, typing. They prioritize what we are attracted to and barely register what we find irrelevant. We move seamlessly from sight to perception, from the information available to the assignment of value and meaning to what we see. We don't see ourselves perceiving. We just see. This means we can be blind about our seeing. Just as sight is not neutral, it is not comprehensive. That is, physical sight goes only so far; it does not include what is invisible. Of course, it is true that the visible signs we receive often give us information about what is invisibly present, but that is by inference and may or may not be accurate. So, beyond the typical range of limitations is the fact that we cannot see or know someone else's heart. That is a fundamental and profound limitation in our sight. Out of sight, out of mind, out of heart—indeed.

What might be the most important thing we would want to know about someone else, we cannot actually see. Just as important, neither can they. We can see behavior and attempt to make correlations to the person's heart and intentions, desires and hopes. If there were a chest window through which we could see our own and one another's heart, we would be no better off. Because the "heart" we want to see is not visible: "The LORD does not see as mortals see; they look on the outward appearance, but the LORD looks on the heart" (1 Sam 16:7). Therefore, we are at least partially blind to our perceiving and partially blind to seeing our perceiving. Sight is no simple matter, and perception makes sight seem like a walk in the park. As plain as can be turns out not to be.

Reflection. How acute is your attention to the world of need around you? To things and people beyond your immediate concern or attention? In what ways are you and are you not a person who actively pays attention to more than your circumstances as you walk through life each day? When you look back on the last forty-eight hours, what details of people and of lives not your own can you list? Describe someone you know who is especially attentive. How do you respond to their example?

VISION VERSUS SIGHT

When I was in recovery from a serious bike accident that nearly blinded me in one eye, I had hours and days to meditate on the meaning and qualities of sight. Over the course of a year, through access to four unusually good, extremely specialized eye surgeries, I gradually came to the point where I could see well again out of both my eyes. In the quiet lull of the weeks just after these operations, I was grateful beyond words that the prospect of normal was hopeful, however tedious the process. What slowly became clear to me was that, as much as I longed for restored sight, I had a need that was deeper, actually beyond surgical reach. More than sight, I needed vision. That is, I needed a change in perception, not just in visual acuity. I needed more than the information gained through sight could deliver to me. If I was going to see the world in the love and mercy of Jesus Christ, and perceive the people and needs of the world in a way that was truthful, then I needed to see with the heart of Jesus. No surgeon could give me this.

As my sight was incrementally restored, I prayed that my heart would be more and more conformed to the One who sees truly. This absence or distortion of vision that comes out of our hearts is the ordinary soil of injustice. As long as you and I see myopically, through the broken glasses of our ordinary lives, then the bedrock of justice has yet to be laid solidly. From poor vision inevitably follows the tragic error of misnaming. To walk by sight is not enough. To walk by faith (in One who is unseen) means we gain the capacity and willingness to see what matters so much to the heart of God. Those people our culture treats as invisible, God sees clearly. In time the invisible God transforms our hearts to see and respond to what and to whom God sees so visibly and lovingly.

I remember a crossroads in my own self-perception. I was savagely self-critical on the one hand, but on the other, I had come to trust the God who said I was "fearfully and wonderfully made" (Ps 139:14). If I listened to my voice, I was defeated before I began. If I listened to what I believed was God's voice, I was free. So which was going to be the more defining truth in my life? Both would probably be with me as long as I lived, but whose voice was going to be the primary voice in my heart? I realized I could, and had to, decide. My life would be the story of which voice I trusted more. I chose then, and most days since, to trust the voice of the One who knows me best.

"To do justice, and to love kindness, and to walk humbly with your God" (Mic 6:8) involves acknowledgment of our need for a new heart and for a set of lifestyle choices essential to gain the vision that reflects the taxonomy of God's heart. Both are needed. They occur in varying order, but they are each essential.

If every taxonomy names and classifies based on what botanists or zoologists see as shared features, God's taxonomy sees each of us as we are, individually and collectively. Because he does so with truth, love and justice, our personal and interpersonal taxonomy needs to be recast by the taxonomy of God. Worship must involve practices of daily life that help us rehearse again and again the open, loving, sacrificial heart of our God who sees and hears the needy.

Reflection. *Sight is how you see. Vision is how you see and your interpretation of what you see. What factors most significantly affect your vision of people around you? of people in need? of global suffering? of individuals who are victims of violence and oppression?*

Self-Seeing

Each of us takes our own journey in this process, which has both predictable and mysterious qualities.

Much of who I am seems predictable, based on aspects of my background. At the same time, I don't understand all of why, for example, self-esteem has been one of my life's great plagues. Especially as a child, teenager, college student and younger adult, the way I saw and failed to see myself was one of my life's painful challenges. This was so despite being raised by loving, indeed doting, parents and surrounded by a caring and gentle extended family. I had a safe, supportive world, but my sense of myself in the world was marked by deep insecurity and personal deficiency. This led me to feel that my life was about overcoming my inadequacies, trying to fill in the gaps, trying to hide or make up for what I wasn't, trying to succeed by success which, of course, didn't work.

MY OWN BROKEN MIRROR

This false sense of myself meant that in the process I came to see others falsely too. I reflected the distortions of my sense of self on them, with varying force and effect. Their responses fed my perceptions and misperceptions. I remember vividly wondering as a child how other children saw themselves in light of what I saw as their greater intelligence, skill, wealth, athleticism or whatever it was that I thought distinguished them. Did they see themselves in the gifted or privileged way I saw them, and did not see myself? Did they consider themselves actually better than others, which is how I saw them, or was that part of their personas? It was all part of how I was learning to see them but also learning to see myself. The external mirrors that friends and teachers provided me reflected positive images, but the mirror of my self-perception was already cracked, so I received even that affirmation through my own broken pattern. Day after day. I could never be or do enough to be right enough.

My personal narrative is just a small expression of one person's experience in a world of six and a half billion people. In some stories the cracks in their mirrors can be much bigger and deeper, and the pieces missing or distorted can be even more dramatically so. But it contributes to a basic fact: we see as we have been seen, or as we think we have been seen. The shattered mirror by which we see ourselves, our neighbors and God affects our hearts' perceptions of everyone and everything else. Add to it stories of abuse, family violence, poverty, gender inequality, drug use, sexism, racism, tribalism and it is not difficult to understand how injustice simply is.

The ubiquitousness of injustice can make it seem benign. That's the problem.

The inescapability of this distorted perception means that we take it for granted as simply a reflection of what is natural and unavoidable. No one is free from this condition. Our perspectives are not only limited and finite, but also distorted and prejudiced. It means that we grow up with greater and lesser measures of awareness, sensitivity and empathy. It can mean that someone else's unjust suffering is someone else's, period. It isn't *mine*. It's evidence of the injustice that corrupts the heart, and it is as common as breathing.

> **Reflection.** *What has cracked or broken your mirror? Why? What has the impact been? How has the grace of God helped you face this and seek God's renewing change in your own life, and in your capacity to mirror the worth of others to them?*

BEYOND THE SOCIAL BELL CURVE

If we see as we are seen, we're in trouble. A false reflection might, for example, overinflate our self-image like a convex mirror, making us appear far taller than we are. We become an elongated, narrow object of attention and think we occupy far more space in the world than we do. Then we easily come to expect others to make room for our large self in the world, letting us swing ourselves into place as our wishes, desires or expectations lead us to do. Our distorted sense of self can leave us feeling entirely unself-conscious about making claims for our view of reality and in turn the way we come to see others around us. We think we are just operating in a way that fits who we are.

Some mirrors are concave and leave us with the emotional impression that we are wider than we are. The girl with the eating disorder thinks she is overweight, even when her hips cannot hold up her pants and her thighs are like toothpicks. Out of obsessive fear of being seen as heavy, she experiences the shame and offensiveness of her disease because she feels compelled to change her appearance so she can see herself as she wants to be seen. The downward spiral is intense and the possibilities few. The hall of mirrors confirms again and again that she can see only as she is sure she is being seen. Similar social patterns can flow from other mirror reflections. To be seen as beautiful by others can open doors like few other qualifications. The pleasure and impressiveness of physical beauty can lead others—whose mirrors may not reflect so beautifully—to withdraw, to adore, to associate, to grovel, to fear.

A person so seen, who then sees the world as one who is seen as beautiful, walking through the day of ordinary life, will see the world around them in a way very different from someone who is seen as plain, unbeautiful, or not seen at all.

This is surely the experience of those seen as odd, different, other. They reflect back into their world the knowledge they believe they have received from how they have been seen in physical appearance, disability, distinctive features, social behavior, speech pattern, racial background, social class. Those social messages are forceful and memorable. They shape the lens through which those judged as "different" see and engage their world. Although some might live in reaction to the visions reflected back upon them, many simply accept and submit to them—true or false, just or unjust.

This creates something like a social bell curve for what is broadly and locally attractive, acceptable and desirable.

"Normal" is the bubble in the middle; irrelevant, unwanted or both are on the extremes. For those outside this bell curve, life is a lot harder. Darken the skin, separate the eyes, flatten the nose, broaden the speech, impoverish the home, and most often one slides farther toward the edges of the bell curve, farther away from being one who gets attention, value, validation, especially if measured by the dominant bell curve of Caucasian culture in the United States.

Recently, as other passengers and I were about to board an airplane, the airline staff called for any needing extra time to board the plane first. Three families with young children, two older people in wheelchairs and one enormously heavy woman stepped up. I wondered for a moment why this woman had come to the front of the line as she shouted back at a friend to bring her something she had left on her seat while waiting. She walked vigorously enough, without aid of any kind. She offered no explanation for why she came forward for early boarding. Then it dawned on me. She didn't need one: it was obvious—her disability was her size. She was significantly outside the physical bell curve. It happened that I sat in the row behind her, and I watched as nearly every other person who came onto the plane looked at her and chose another row. It was astounding how consistent this was, as more than one hundred people registered in unmistakable ways that this woman was outside the standard deviation. It was not done with conscious cruelty or with mean intent. Of course, they may have simply been looking for more room, but their faces told a more complex and judgmental story.

We know the bell curves and we readily use them. How much more powerfully excluding, then, can crosscultural distinctions be? Here the angles of refraction send even more forceful imprinting images. Some can be exotic and attractive, alluring and affirming, welcoming and inclusive. But for many people, "other" is almost always bad and problematical, if not life-threatening. It conveys not just odd but less, not just different but inferior, not just unfamiliar but undesired, not just questionable but unwanted. Then, as we imagine all that crosscultural distinction, combine it with extreme poverty, no sanitation, no education, no water. What you have is possibly so far beyond the bell curve of what registers as important, valuable or attractive that there is very little for those in the middle of the bell curve to see or to care about.

A friend was recently seated on an airplane immediately in front of an Iraqi family that was being relocated from the East to the West Coast by United Nations staff. The father, the mother, the two small children and the grandfather were late in being seated, awkwardly interrupting the expectations of the surrounding passengers. That none of this family spoke English, that the children were obviously scared and untutored in the basics of flying etiquette, that they carried a pungent aroma from their travels, and that the grandfather had no legs all added to the drama. The family showed the signs of being in painful trauma. What the nearby passengers were riled over were some moments, maybe even some hours, of what by contrast was surely not what the Iraqi family was facing. But, my friend reported, you would have thought the other passengers were experiencing the greater suffering.

Meanwhile it does not register that within this pattern are revelations of what comes out of the heart. Each day we think we are just benignly walking into the social landscape. In what seems to be an innocuous, ordinary, commonplace set of misperceptions lies the selfish soil that allows daily injustice to thrive, especially for those beyond the bell curve. In even casual strolls down the street or the grocery store aisle, we order the social universe in accordance with our hearts.

> *Reflection.* What is the bell curve of your social relationships? What type of people fit where in your social awareness? Draw a bell curve of those who matter in your social environment and those who matter to the kingdom of God. How similar and different are these lists? Why?

THE BIBLE AND THE BROKEN MIRROR

It takes no more than two chapters from "the beginning" in the Bible before the pattern of misperception, the shattered mirror by which we fail to see God, ourselves and our neighbor, becomes the human norm. By looking at the narrative line of Genesis alone, we find the tragic story of how a distorted refraction of our broken humanity is reproduced again and again (Gen 1–11; 30–58). Adam, a reflection of *imago Dei*, encounters through the serpent a shadow that alters and distorts the light of his Creator. What had been the liberty of going anywhere in the Garden was replaced in Adam's and Eve's imaginations by the temptation of the boundary not to eat of one tree. What had been vast and open suddenly became small and desperate, expressly out of the serpent's inference that God either didn't want Adam and Eve's freedom, or didn't trust their power. A lie turned into a deception. That distortion of the *imago Dei*, and all its implications, has been with us ever since.

In the mirror of Adam's first exclamation to Eve we see the radiance of human communion and intimacy. The serpent's temptation and Adam's and Eve's subsequent choice are like a rock thrown at what had been whole ("This at last is bone of my bones and flesh of my flesh"), shattering it into shards of blame ("the woman whom you gave to be with me"). Those who had seen each other naked and unashamed now hid—from God and from one another. Cain and Abel capture the spirit of seeing themselves and each other wrongly and prejudicially. Though brothers, one comes to see his brother as foe, competitor, enemy, and calibrates all of life on the basis of those lies. Desperate to correct or alter what we know is wrong about our image in another's eyes, we ironically enact what they are showing us, all the while fighting to reveal that we are someone else. The text notes that, before the flood, God sees "that every inclination of the thoughts of their hearts was only evil continually. And the LORD was sorry that he had made humankind on the earth, and it grieved him to his heart" (Gen 6:5-6). To call this condition a shattered mirror seems, if anything, understated.

The story of Joseph adds to our understanding of this destructive paradigm. The youngest son is isolated into insignificance as a shepherd because of the jealousy of his older siblings. They couldn't stand seeing the shine in their father Jacob's eye for Joseph. That sets the whole sad tale in motion. The blind favoritism of Jacob justifies the blind disdain of his siblings. Since Joseph is perceived as a threat, an impediment, a problem, they determine to do what they feel is justified: remove him. By putting his life in danger, but without killing him, they could rationalize the legitimacy of their actions without feeling fully liable for the extent of the consequences.

This is often just where we choose to live: perceiving in self-justifying ways, we frame our conviction in words that prescribe meanings for the sake of our desired outcomes, and then take actions that push things to go our way without leaving any trail of guilt or accusation. The roommate spat had to do with them, not really me (and my habits, choices, attitude). The marriage ended because of her (or his) anger issues, and my behavior was incidental. The job came to an end because of a lousy boss, that was all. We can claim all these as acts of injustice, in fact.

What makes the Joseph story noteworthy, however, is that despite how shrewdly and powerfully his brothers weighted things to tell Joseph one message about himself, a message that often debilitates someone, Joseph came to perceive and name it all differently. That may be a function of the years of reflection he eventually had in captivity, not the moment he was left for dead. Much later in his story, Joseph came to understand the message of his brothers loud and clear: by what they did they "intended to do harm to [Joseph]." But God intended it differently in Joseph's understanding, "for good, in order to preserve a numerous people, as he is doing today." Joseph went on to tell his brothers, "So have no fear; I myself will provide for you and your little ones" (Gen 50:20-21). The blessing was for Joseph and for far more than Joseph. He operated out of God's frame rather than the one handed him by his brothers.

Joseph looked into the mirror that was God's image of him and of them. It changed everything. It was the difference between injustice and grace. The Bible is as replete with stories of our broken mirrors as is history itself. The ministry of Jesus is a ministry of recasting how we see the world. The frames we use are ever present and flawed. That's true for how we see or don't see the leper (Mt 8), the woman with the flow of blood who touched Jesus' garment (Lk 8), Zacchaeus (Lk 19), the woman who breaks her alabaster jar to anoint Jesus (Mt 26) and others. This is what makes Jesus so troubling to those around him. They don't see, and don't want to see, the way Jesus does.

In one of the later books of the New Testament, we are told that

God's law is like a mirror that shows us who we are to be and how we are to see, but it cannot transform us into such people. James captures it this way:

> Be doers of the word, and not merely hearers who deceive themselves. For if any are hearers of the word and not doers, they are like those who look at themselves in a mirror; for they look at themselves and, on going away, immediately forget what they were like. But those who look into the perfect law, the law of liberty, and persevere, being not hearers who forget but doers who act—they will be blessed in their doing. (Jas 1:22-25)

Our incapacity to remember to do the right thing distorts our capacity to see the right thing as well. In failing to act justly we show we have lost our call to see clearly. If we cannot see ourselves, we are going to be all the more distorted in our vision of our neighbor and of God. That's how the story of injustice turns out.

Reflection. *How does this theme in the Bible help you see yourself? What common or different threads strike you? Why? Do you see yourself as an insider or as an outsider to the Bible's portrait of our brokenness? Why?*

The Crux

Tribal custom can create a lost life for widows of AIDS in places like Uganda, Zambia and Kenya. Typically HIV is the "gift" of the husband. Counter to most national laws, when a woman is widowed, the home she and her children live in becomes the property of the husband's family. In thousands of cases this means that the desperation of families will cause them to move into the widow's home and "land grab," kicking out the widow and her children, leaving them homeless and resourceless. While most African countries have laws against this practice of land grabbing, a vulnerable, possibly HIV-infected widow is typically seen as nobody, and she is not even acknowledged enough to be named as the victim that she is. In the terms that you and I would consider the most basic decency, she is lost and forgotten. This common poison can destroy the woman and her children.

COMPASSIONATE DISPASSION

As one who lives in a country where the rule of law exists, and where most can access a legal advocate for assistance, I can hear about the problem of land grabbing in Africa and think of it with compassionate dispassion. It's a distant problem, a domestic issue, an injustice to be sure. But knowing about it, finding it tragic and wrong, is not the same as actually coming close to the situation, let alone engaging the real people in it. It's another "starving child," but not, so to speak, "my starving child."

My view of this changed when I met Esther, one such displaced widow. The chances still exist that I can treat this as her issue, but the possibilities are substantially diminished as I hear her story, watch her tears, feel her sadness and anguish for her children and herself. The real person erases the distant filtered image. Esther is not the same as a "victim of land grabbing."

The chances are, however, that most of the land-grabbing victims will not get such notice. Unseen, unnamed, they simply suffer. A widow may sit and nurse her often HIV-positive infant from her undernourished body while millions like us are glued to *American Idol* or some other version of "reality TV." We live with a misaligned passion, feeling we have few resources to change things and thinking that there is so little we can do. Either we typically don't know about or see such widows at all, or we do but our hearts misperceive them and wrap their vulnerable lives in a legal category or a dispassionate reality. Meanwhile, nothing changes. No good is done. No justice is sought. No hope emerges. Another broken looking glass and more poisonous words.

We might think that the images and language we use to frame those who live encumbered by injustice are more or less benign, that seeing and naming things is not really the issue. What I am arguing, however, is that evil arises from the seedbed of our heart and goes on to misname the world, letting injustice exist "out there" while we go on seeing and naming the world in ways that serve our interests.

We leave ourselves out of the equation of needing to learn to see and name differently—with the consequence that we would then have to act differently. This is privilege, whether we know it or call it that or not. It makes us more complicit in the suffering of the world than we want to admit. That's the point. We don't have to. Meanwhile, others suffer while we look through scratched lenses, or shutter our windows and don't look out at all. We then frame our perceptions, blindness or dispassion with words that sustain patterns of injustice and leave us feeling free from any real responsibility. We write ourselves out of the story and thereby out of any relationship with the suffering of others. It's our language game. It serves our ends. It satisfies our conditions. It perpetuates the status of *our* lives. But no more than that. Certainly not learning to do good, or seeking justice (Is 1:17).

> **Reflection.** *Our perceiving can be done from such safe distances that the needs of others make no claim on us. This is part of our lives of privilege. What are the evidences of privilege in your life, especially in your assumptions? What are examples of how privilege shapes your life at this point? Why does it matter to try to understand how basic and different it is to live with privilege? What do you think Jesus says about privilege? What does privilege prevent us from seeing or feeling? Why?*

SALTY MEMORIES

It was the middle of the night when I arrived for the first time in India. As I sat outside the airport in Chennai, there before me, in almost stereotypical guise, were some of "the starving children of India." You know, the children I was told to eat my peas or broccoli for when I was a small child at our family dinner table. No longer mythic, no longer television images. Here were real children in tangible need. It was no guise. I knew, of course, that these ones who had staked out the territory of the airport might be pimped, if not enslaved. They also might actually be doing better than some other beggar children. They might actually have had limbs severed specifically for the sake of intensifying their appearance in order to increase their earning power. But, in any case, they were real children, in real need, however complex the unknown backdrop of their lives might be. The starving children of India were now before me, and I was still, in part, on the other side of the television.

The scene felt both familiar and surreal. There was no screen to turn away from, let alone turn off. But I couldn't emotionally access these children all that easily either. I had had children in Seattle beg from me before. This was both like that and not like that at all. I played with them some, laughed as they furtively came close, then skipped or darted away. Their eyes were those of children, but their gestures were more experienced than they should have been. The moment was both present and distant, and so were the children. They were in my world and I was in theirs, yet none of us was in either.

I wondered if I seemed fictional to them: someone with my skin color, without the wear of the sun, who arrived from somewhere and landed on their terrain like a visitor from space. All this to say, I bore the signs of someone who was not like them, who was not in their (shoeless) circumstances. I might be willing and able to give them some money. What was most real about me was that I fit the profile within the moving cast of bodies who makes it possible for them to eat or to survive. Whatever fiction I may have been to them, these children were real and unreal to me. The scene was so like its documentary imagery that those first moments in India already felt like déjà vu. I could only imagine what I did not know about their young lives. I wonder still today if they have survived. If they have, what made it possible for them to do so? What work? What inner resolve? What good fortune? What daily struggles?

"At risk" was a label I had never heard at the time, but surely it would have been an accurate description based on some of the threats or dangers in their lives. It would probably have added to other categories and adjectives I already had for them: poor, hungry, filthy, shoeless, scrawny, sprightly, alone. Such words have never been applied to my life, nor to my brother, nor to my wife, nor to my children. We, after all, are on this side of things, and these children were on that side.

From that same trip, I can recall many other snapshots that have affected my heart. One is of some street children I had the chance to meet, to talk with (albeit through a translator) and to listen to as carefully as I could. I heard them describe their day, their dwelling, their responsibilities and some of their fears. This knowledge was unforgettable, not because the details were surprising but because it was this or that child's actual life.

Another scene I remember too was gradually coming to see through the mist and smoke of a southern Indian village the forms of several men, each asleep on successive steps, wrapped on a chilly night in a single, very thin cloth. It's easy to recall at this moment the smell, sound and look of those in need at the Kali Temple in Calcutta, near the site of Mother Teresa's Missionaries of Charity—the dirt and chaos everywhere outside the entrance, contrasting with the calm and cleanliness inside the doors. I have traveled to India to meet *Dalit* brothers and sisters in Christ and to hear them tell of being born (by force of caste) into a life of cleaning latrines—their only alternative for work and food.

In the end, and again today, my heart was snatched by those dancing children of many years ago, and by other children and adults I have met. I have traveled to many places not to be an agent of change but because I need to be changed. Gratefully, these children and adults have been among the catalysts that continue to alter the alchemy of my heart, to affect my assumptions. They have been part of God's answer to my prayer that that first trip to India would present me with images and impressions I simply could not get out of my heart and mind, but would have to see and feel and remember and respond to the rest of my life.

Reflection. In what ways have you come near to people in pain or experiencing injustice? How have such situations affected you? How penetrating or heart-changing were those experiences? How do they or don't they daily shape your heart?

MATTERS OF IDENTITY

The urgency of injustice could not be greater than when it is experienced every day. Until our hearts allow this ordinary daily reality to enter our lives with some degree of the same empathic force it would if the injustice were against us or against those we most love, then the chances of a more just world become very dim.

In the hills bordering Thailand and Myanmar live tribal people without any legal identity. That is, they are not officially recognized persons and therefore are perceived to be without any entitlement to the rule of law or to any other provisions of citizenry, such as the potential ownership of land or police protection. In that sense, they do not exist. They are not citizens, and there are thousands of them. This situation exists as a result of complex political reasons that serve the ends of the Thai government. Seen as nobodies, they are named nothing, which is a kind of legal, social, political and economic death. As long as they are not really seen, and as long as they do not have any real name (identity, citizenship, etc.), they can be handled, dispensed with, in whatever way the government chooses. It is the story of a totally encompassing vulnerability. It therefore is a story of life and death daily for those who live as nobodies in northern Thailand. This is not a benign, bureaucratic legal snafu. It's a strategy of political, economic and social abuse. If they are recognized and legitimized as citizens, there are consequences. To change their status costs someone money. To leave them, ignore them, abuse them, deny them costs less. How close are we willing to let such people come into our lives?

Many of these refugees are now being resettled, from Thailand and from many other nations, and are now next door "over there"— they clean our clothes, our homes, our cars. They ride next to us on the freeway. They attend our children's schools. We may treat or see them as "other" but they are no longer distant.

A few years ago my identity was stolen, and thousands of dollars of computers were purchased on illegal credit cards gained through the use of my social security number. I became aware of this when a national credit agency representative reached me by telephone one morning. Suddenly, out of the blue, this man I did not know, after a minimal and slurred introduction, started hammering me on the phone about my failure to pay my bills, and told me that unless I did so immediately, legal action would be taken. It took three years to sort out all the complexities and hassles of this.

In the end I could use many of the privileges of my life (being educated, male, articulate, determined, connected) to be able to demonstrate that the charges were false, that they had nothing to do with me and that my identity should be restored, and it was. And still—and still—I was aware in the midst of this process that I felt as if I was seen as nobody and named as nobody. And that's as a person with great privilege in a nation with the rule of law and the resources to make the law do its work on my behalf. None of that is available or true for the hill tribe people of northern Thailand.

Reflection. My identity matters to me far more than my neighbor's does. Fair enough. But why does our suffering neighbor's identity matter so little to us? Why is it so discretionary that we are very slow, even passive, in responding to their crisis? What is it about my identity that lets me live so comfortably with such dissonance and need?

FIELD OF VISION

Experience affects how far and wide and well we see the world around us. Our capacity for sight is not all the same, for starters, and is no doubt affected by temperament, mental abilities and exposure. Beyond these basic factors, however, are the experiences of a person's life. To be raised in East Oakland, in one of the most violent neighborhoods in Northern California, is not going to be a neutral experience for anyone learning to see their neighbors, near or far. To have been to many funerals of your teenage peers killed in gang violence is not going to mean that you see the world clearly, even if you do learn to see its brutality. In fact, the deep scratches of that brutality can make your vision of it seem normal. As a result, many of the survivors don't expect to live that long, and they see others around them in ways that fit that expectation. Lives are seen to be worthless. Safety is worth something, but not as much as the next drug deal or your loyalty to your gang. Danger means survival more than it does threat. Their experience of seeing etches a field of vision that explains events, relationships, encounters. In different ways and to different degrees, they are both victims and victimizers.

Yet all seers are both victims and victimizers in different ways and to different degrees. Fei, for a different example, was raised as an immigrant child in a family for whom she was the primary English speaker. She grew up in constantly changing locations, expected from a young age to be her parents' interpreter in official appointments with doctors or others. Her family's life depended on what she understood and said. The pressure, anxiety, frequency of it left significant marks on how she sees the world: filled with lots of people who consistently are older, bigger, more verbal, male, aggressive and powerful. Then there is everyone else. Then there is Fei. She does not see herself or others through a neutral lens, but rather through one that has been scratched in particular and profound ways.

Raymond is a forty-year-old man who has deep emotional wounds from his childhood that leave him without any clear sense of identity. This makes it all the more surprising that his way of engaging the world comes up to but seldom ever crosses the threshold of letting such wounds be suspected. People who encounter him experience him as confident, clear, determined, but with little or no edge of aggression that might make one think of him as an overcompensating strider. Yet from what he tells me, all this has to be chosen as an act of the will because his actual perception of himself and of others is so distorted. It's like relational Braille.

One woman I know sees the world through the experience of daily incest for almost a decade of her life. A young boy I know carried the family hope for a better day since he was the only one who made it through school. An apparently wealthy woman I know struggles to find enough money to feed her family. A buoyant young adult I know cuts herself in panic and self-loathing. A teenager I know is trying to figure out what to do about all his new feelings now that puberty is in full force and he sees girls in a way he never has before. A friend who is dying is going back to look again at a broken family system that he helped break and is trying to see his way toward healing before he is gone. A young teenager I met lived for his first ten years in a dislocation camp in northern Uganda and for five of those had to sleep away from his parents every night in order to keep from being forced to be a child soldier. A loving young woman who has had several years of infertility now sees her friends and their babies through tears and anger. Someone who already had learned that life is often Plan B now sees it as Plan E, and the way he looks at everyone and everything around is changed.

To do justice requires holding injustice clearly, unmistakably, urgently in our field of vision.

Reflection. If no one sees with full clarity, what do you look for in the faces of others? How hard or easy is it for you to read signs of the pain in others' lives? How do you respond when you see it? What does it take for you to open your heart to them and their need? What do you make of that fact?

DEPTH PERCEPTION

We see shallowly. We typically project onto others' lives what fits the scenarios we craft for them. This is not, of course, just an act of our eyes but a matter of our hearts. Empathy, our capacity to perceive and at least partially enter into someone else's reality, comes with a price. Often we are not interested in paying it. So we just see with our eyes, and frankly, they don't take us all that far.

We nonetheless rely on cultural categories and patterns to inform what we observe, infer, deduce and conclude about one another. Research about perception has gone into many different lines of consideration, from the impact of symmetry in a person's facial structure to the relative prominence of eyes, cheekbones, jaws, teeth, hair and so on. We almost instantaneously read, analyze, prioritize and evaluate cues about a person's attractiveness.

I don't know John's condition, nor is it easy to describe. He is personable, honest, immediate, warm—and awkward. He does not have a job or show signs that he will be getting one. Something is amiss in his mind, but not quite. Something seems peculiar about his way of relating; he moves in too close too quickly, especially with young adult women, and yet is not so much threatening as just too much.

John is an earnest Christian. I had run into him at one of his local haunts, a café he frequents most days, where everyone knows him by name. On this day John quickly connected with a friend of his who was accompanied by his guide dog. It seemed they had intended to meet, and after John helped his friend to a table and got settled, he placed his order. Midway in their conversation, he went back to the service counter. As he did so, he stopped to talk to a young woman accompanied by her mother. John stood too close. He looked at her too directly. He assumed a posture that was invisible and unnoticed by his blind friend, but for the seeing world, not least for this young woman, was clearly awkward. The mother moved closer, sending a signal John did not read. After the brief exchange with John was over, she came closer still, and mother and daughter looked plaintively into each other's eyes as the mother gently stroked her daughter's hair. No audible comment passed between them, but many passed silently. John failed to see. But his failed vision of others and himself means he gets the same in return.

My own blindness is different from John's. I, for example, don't see as well as I might because I see as a person who is white. One evening our pastoral staff asked for the privilege of gathering with about fifteen men and women for a candid discussion about their experience of life as African Americans. It was a profound gift to sit with these brothers and sisters in Christ, representing three generations, and hear them simply describe daily life in the San Francisco Bay area as African Americans. Our only objective for the evening was to hear them share their stories. They told us how they see themselves and the varied, complex, often shocking and painful ways they are seen and interacted with as African Americans: the constant effects of informal and formal racial profiling they experience, even in the "enlightened" East Bay. How important to see through the eyes of these friends. Our pastoral staff had some racial diversity, and serving our multiracial church had made them reasonably alert to these realities. Still, what we saw that night was how little and how shallowly we see. Deep pain can be caused by our shallow vision of others.

Apartheid constitutionalized shallow vision. By it, the South African government essentially said, "Let's commit ourselves as a nation to seeing superficially and prejudicially. By looking on the surface, let's see what we can find through personal appearance, and then place each person in one of several arbitrary categories of distinction and separation into which each will be imprisoned. This will be our national life." The history of apartheid is the story of what happens when this shallowness is enforced upon a whole population as the definition of what is allowed.

More recently, Rwandan killed Rwandan during the 1994 genocide: Hutus killing Tutsis. On the basis of what seemed to many Western eyes as being almost indistinguishable differences between these rather arbitrarily assigned tribal identities (given by Belgian colonial authorities), lives were lost, nearly a million lives in eight weeks. Tribal identity can be definitional, but for most in Rwanda it was not. It could be named, and for some it was important, but not for vast numbers of people. Yet from that superficial category of identity, untold suffering and pain followed. As the Rwandan genocide unfolded, it was superficially discounted by an inference that it was "just those Africans having another war." The international community seemed to see it as neither urgent enough nor angst-driven enough. By their inaction, the shallow vision of the white Western world reflected back to black Africans that their suffering and crisis were not ours. Tragedy. Injustice.

> **Reflection.** *Choose one primary global issue of need (e.g., Israel-Palestine, Congo, Pakistan-India, child slavery, bonded labor, sex trafficking) or choose one person you have contact with who is at the margins of justice (e.g., a homeless person, a panhandler, etc.). Track this area's or person's needs daily through whatever means you can (conversation, personal visits, Internet, prayer, books, reflection, imagination, etc.). How deep are you willing to go in entering another person's reality and need? What stops you? paralyzes you?*

THE KEY TO MY NEIGHBOR'S HOUSE

Genocide gives us a horrific look at our human capacity to live with shuttered windows, shuttered vision of even desperate need. Given the right circumstances, loyalties between neighbors can break open along previously incidental or invisible lines of distinction. In a flash those who were only the people next door can become our enemy; they become our victim or we theirs. As recently as 1994 the story of the Rwandan genocide took at least a few weeks to actually arrive clearly in the lives of even the most informed people in the United Nations and in the United States. Eventually there was complete clarity, but even then the international response was dramatically inadequate and inept. We had a capacity to keep the shutters closed, knowing that to look was to see something unimaginable.

In Bosnia, during approximately the same time, for related and parallel reasons, another genocide was unfolding on European soil, perhaps over an even more tortured political landscape. A powerful book by Elizabeth Neuffer, *The Key to My Neighbor's House: Seeking Justice in Bosnia and Rwanda*, opens with a testimony from which she gets her title. The testimony of Hamdo Kahrimanović before the International Criminal Tribunal for the former Yugoslavia includes this exchange:

> "I do not know that you could give me a complete answer, but perhaps you can help me to understand since I am not from that area. How could you explain some of the atrocities that we have heard that have been committed? . . . Given your background, your experiences, knowing that Serbs and Muslims lived together, went to school together, how did that happen?" asked Judge Gabrielle Kirk McDonald of the witness before her in the first international war crimes trial since World War II.
>
> Hamdo paused. "It is difficult to answer, this question," he replied. "I am also at a loss. I had the key to my next-door neighbor's [house] who was a Serb, and he had my key. That is how we looked after each other."

"That is how we looked after each other." And then, we came to look at each other in a completely different way. Behind shuttered windows, etched lenses, shattered mirrors are our vulnerable, fearful, self-justifying hearts. As Neuffer later observes, after meeting briefly with one of the especially cruel men in Serbia:

The evil I glimpsed in him had nothing to do with ideology; in some ways, if I could have chalked up his actions to a kind of nationalist brainwashing, I would not have felt so disturbed. . . . The evil I glimpsed in him was the potential for evil we all share, for being human is no guarantee of our humanity. What's most chilling when you meet a murderer is that you meet yourself.[1]

We don't have to encounter evil this virulent in order for our hearts to reveal that what we don't want to see in the world is also what we sometimes don't want to see in ourselves. We don't want to see *there* what we don't want to see *here* either. Everywhere we look and everything we see we perceive from a biased heart. Our fear, apprehension and distortion of what we see are ubiquitous. This includes our attempts at not seeing, at shuttering the windows. But not seeing, like not deciding, is an act of its own. It's the option of the ostrich burying its head—and that is hardly the incarnation, the evidence of God seeing and entering our needy world in human flesh.

> **Reflection.** *How do you respond to Neuffer's statement "What's most chilling when you meet a murderer is that you meet yourself"? Do you find yourself instinctively accepting or denying that statement? Why? Do you find the horrors of others imaginable within your heart? How so?*

DIMNESS

For now we see in a mirror, dimly, but then we will see face to face. Now I know only in part; then I will know fully, even as I have been fully known. (1 Cor 13:12)

---

[1]Elizabeth Neuffer, *The Key to My Neighbor's House: Seeking Justice in Bosnia and Rwanda* (New York: Picador, 2001), p. xiii.

We are fully seen by God, but we do not fully see God. Paul, who was seen by the risen Jesus on the road to Damascus, was transformed by God's vision of him (which included God's perception that to persecute the church was to persecute Jesus himself). God saw what no one else did. This is the story of God's promise, the transformation of one heart at a time. It's the slow process of living in the hope of one day seeing face to face. It's the longing of knowing as we have been known. That hope is not fulfilled today. Nor has it yet been any day. Between now and then, however, the life and work of God's people is the ministry of seeing and living by faith. "Seeing through a glass darkly" gives us enough sight but not all we need; we can see (and we are not left in darkness and agnosticism), but we see in part (we are not seeing clearly or fully). This underlines why the basic issues of our broken mirrors, etched lenses and shuttered windows have to be taken so seriously. It's why we have to resist our presumption to name what we think we see when we ought to be clear that to do so requires wisdom we do not have. Even when we may think we "get it" we often don't. That's not easy to admit but is essential to stay open. We are led to humble ourselves before the One whose heart, vision and naming produce life, when ours does not. We are meant to look again, to see anew, to pay attention, to name in truth, and to act in love and justice.

All this starts, ends and is sustained in a lifestyle of worship. This life of waking up to God and the full love and justice God has for the world on any and every day. We have to learn to move, to think, to act, to feel anew what it means to follow the passions of God for a broken world. Every small and large way we do that is a mirror of God's love in our life of worship individually and corporately. It is then the reflection of the God whose love sees and holds us all. When we gather weekly in corporate worship, it's the refinement and collection of our daily worship that welcomes us, forgives and heals us, calls us, and sends us to live our worship again.

For reasons I don't understand, the backlight on my computer monitor will sometimes just gradually dim. I barely seem to notice it until under some condition it seems very clear just how dark the screen has become, and I go in and adjust the setting. It is not unusual for the light to be less than a quarter of full strength, which is where I prefer it to be. I have almost no idea that it has diminished, and certainly no idea that it is so low. I can see enough, sufficiently and then some. But that is nothing like what I see after I have made the adjustment. To make the simple point: I didn't see what I didn't see.

That is the story of our lives. What complicates the picture further is the fact that I am in a world that rewards selective, privileged, reinforcing vision, not a vision that calls what is being seen as incomplete or misleading or self-serving or a lie. We are willing to get by with seeing what we do. The gospel wants to readjust the setting so we come to see all we can see (which of course is still dimmer than the full reality). When the light goes up on my computer screen, I am relieved. I can feel my face relaxing because I am no longer inadvertently squinting. But when I come to see the world of great need and pain more vividly and fully, I am not relaxed. It complicates my life. It forces me to ponder and feel and explore far more than I would have to do otherwise. It makes me wonder what else I don't see. It creates an urgency to do something about what I now see. The dimmer screen has its advantages, and truth and justice are not among them. To see better, if still dimly, is essential to changing the way I live. Especially if I want to live loving God and my neighbor.

Reflection. *How are you encouraged by God's desire to help you see and respond to our world less dimly? Do you like seeing more clearly and brightly? What are the costs? How can this journey for you be helped by others doing the same?*

Sabbath Encouragement

It's time again to pause, to take a break from the work of these reflections and again be refreshed by remembering God, whose perceptions of us and of our world constitute the ground of all our hope. Why shouldn't we stop and admit being overwhelmed by our misperceiving hearts and just give up? Because even at this moment we are already seen by the heart of God in Christ as we are meant to come and see one another.

We are as changed by God's gaze as others may come, in part, to be changed by ours. This well-known text is the picture of love through which we are loved in Jesus Christ. It is meant to be a description of the love others are to receive from us in Jesus' name.

> If I speak in the tongues of mortals and of angels, but do not have love, I am a noisy gong or a clanging cymbal. And if I have prophetic powers, and understand all mysteries and all knowledge, and if I have all faith, so as to remove mountains, but do not have love, I am nothing. If I give away all my possessions, and if I hand over my body so that I may boast, but do not have love, I gain nothing.
>
> Love is patient; love is kind; love is not envious or boastful or arrogant or rude. It does not insist on its own way; it is not irritable or resentful; it does not rejoice in wrongdoing, but rejoices in the truth. It bears all things, believes all things, hopes all things, endures all things.
>
> Love never ends. But as for prophecies, they will come to an end; as for tongues, they will cease; as for knowledge, it will come to an end. For we know only in part, and we prophesy only in part; but when the complete comes, the partial will come to an end. When I was a child, I spoke like a child, I thought like a child, I reasoned like a child; when I became an adult, I put an end to childish ways. For now we see in a mirror, dimly, but then we will see face to face. Now I know

only in part; then I will know fully, even as I have been fully known. And now faith, hope, and love abide, these three; and the greatest of these is love. (1 Cor 13)

1. I want again to encourage you to memorize this familiar text so you can better meditate on it. Paul says elsewhere that we should dwell on what is lovely and so forth.

2. I want to encourage you to focus in your sabbath encouragement on the fact that this chapter describes how God sees and loves you. Your vision may be distorted by your heart. But God's is not. Let this be your dwelling place as you rest in your reading, and as you eventually go on to the next section.

3. The greatest hope is that love will triumph, and that is precisely what this text (as do so many others) vigorously affirms.

Take some days just to rest from reading this book. Let it steep. Pray that God will take what is most useful for you and cause it to grow in your heart, and release you from what is not your burden in this season.

PRAYER

Almighty God, to Whom all hearts are open, all desires known, and from Whom no secrets are hidden: cleanse the thoughts of our hearts by the inspiration of Your Holy Spirit, that we may perfectly love You, and worthily magnify Your holy name; through Christ our Lord. Amen.

THE ALTERNATIVE SERVICE BOOK

Part Three

Naming

Choosing Names

Dustin was born with severe cerebral palsy. The doctors told his parents that Dustin "had no hope . . . would not be capable of relationship . . . would never bond." To accept such a prognosis, the doctors went on, was no doubt difficult but right and necessary since it was, after all, just realistic. This, the doctors said, would in turn lead to fairly clear and specific consequences: Dustin should not be taken home; he should live in an institution where there were people who could take care of children like him and his parents and sisters should then get on with their lives. Dustin, they summarized, was a regrettable genetic circumstance. The "names" these doctors gave Dustin and his condition could have framed his entire life. Their names circumscribed Dustin's life. Seen this way, Dustin's life was tragically small.

RENAMING DUSTIN

Dustin's parents and his two sisters, however, had the capacity and readiness to choose other names: son and brother, for starters. From those names, over the past three decades, has come an entirely different set of categories, possibilities, expectations and resources. From those emerged a life-giving set of names necessary to capture Dustin: acute observer, baseball fan, courageous namer, funny guy, philosopher, theologian, writer, disciple, and above all, gift and treasure. The names "son" and "brother" were enough to create a different life for Dustin. Cerebral palsy, after all, was his disability, not his identity. His incapacities did not define his relationships. His parents chose and lived out their names for Dustin because who they loved and what they valued shaped how they saw him and what they did. Their daily acts of naming him, in contrast to the doctors, led to a different life for Dustin and for their family and friends. Dustin's disability made him appear to be someone he was not. The distinct prison of cerebral palsy easily lends itself to this disjunction. The act of naming Dustin for who he is allowed him to then be himself and become himself. Had he been misnamed, potentially neither of those would have been possible.

Dustin's parents saw their son beyond his condition. Dustin cannot speak. He has no ability to communicate orally. His tight and tortured body, however, does not diminish his radiant, if spasmodic, grin. His groans, deliberate and spontaneous, are rich with punctuation and suggestive of content. In time, and with great personal effort through the use of a head stylus and keypad, it gradually became possible for Dustin to be known through written communication.

During the season when I was first getting to know Dustin and his family, his father shared some of Dustin's writing with me. The following essay was written for an online school assignment when Dustin was sixteen. Its profound, distinct images and syntax would not have come to be had Dustin been left misnamed:

My Most Important Decision

It really is like letting very doomed emotions peel like a banana. Issues in my silent mind are causing domineering tiles of negative thoughts to foolishly build. They tempt me to stop working on my noticed strength and not write. Teased by cerebral palsy, it is tempting to give up.

Titled notion, about imagined told would have been emerges as self-pity. If doing time on self-pity roller coaster got any etymology awards my canceled voice would win. Great fool that I am, I get used dissected genuine brain tissue. Tests my ability to laugh.

Emerging in the usual spot in my mind is normality. It is nine sane daring thoughts in a dappled dish.

At manly morning of Good Friday someone heard my worried lost story. He daringly leant me his non-solicited attitude. Barely the action of a tall king, he bailed the world out. Titled Jesus adjusted man's luck.

Borrowed temptation for self-pity ails my soul. Deciding to trust Jesus turns this around. The after tiled wall tumbles. Bright ideas enter my mind. Bit by the love of Jesus, I let nets of sorrowful attitudes escape.

I am a writer. God has given me this ability. I need to remember Easter.

Eternity is my time to run. Now is my time to write.

Without being truthfully named, all this and far more would never have been, or at least been known, about Dustin. It certainly would never have been known that Dustin had any decisions to make, let alone such important ones. It comes down to naming, and why it matters so much.

Reflection. *Let yourself imagine being Dustin. Describe your life if you lived it in Dustin's circumstances. How do you imagine what your heart, mind, soul would be like? Why? Where would you turn for help? Who would you rely on to tell you who you are? Why?*

WRONG NAMES

Our misperceiving leads to our misnaming. We use language, verbal and nonverbal labels, to manage the world around us. We name what we see in terms that reflect value, meaning, position, relationship, affinity. When a human being is mis-seen and then mis-named, the soulish soil of injustice reveals its destructive fertility. What Dustin's doctors were doing seemed benign and honest to them. But they were shortsighted and wrong.

The problem is that you and I name without caution, justification or reason—let alone justice—as we move through life every day. Most naming occurs in ordinary moments. It happens as we respond to fellow drivers, as we stand in line, as we meet people, as we watch TV, as we read the newspaper, as we look at our peers in school. This is not the isolated work of a special class; it is the most ordinary stuff of daily human interaction.

In our names for one another, for better and for worse, lies the evidence of what is in our hearts. Our distorted sight of God, ourselves and our neighbor leads us to name wrongly. We name falsely. It's not that we simply call Beth, Betty. It's that we can call one who is a beloved treasure, trash. When Dustin becomes a "genetic circumstance" he is lost. When Elisabeth is no longer "my sister's daughter," let alone "fearfully and wonderfully made," and becomes instead "a body," "a commodity," "a transaction," "a slave," some*one* has become some*thing*. When Mitali hears that she is "that ugly, black thing," something has shattered. When even "you" becomes a term of disregard, a life of infinite worth is damaged and potentially destroyed.

We hear endless statistics and become weary and paralyzed: 5.7 million children under the age of five die annually, or 1 million children are sold into sex trafficking each year. Then we go on with our consuming life without pause. We hear that the amount we spend on cosmetics in the United States is more than the gross national product of India, and we find our conscience is barely tweaked. We can understand that seven thousand more people will die of AIDS today, but never take a step in response to that pandemic. How can this be? In part it is because of how we name (or don't name) those at the painful end of the crisis. We name so that responsibility is passed to nameless others: "someone should do something for them." Misnaming extends and distills our misperceptions; it frames our consequent inaction and misaction. We manage our weariness and paralysis by names that keep the needs of others distant, our responsibility deflected and our potential power for change untapped.

This is the Bible's story. This is our human tale.

> **Reflection.** *Take steps to become deliberately conscious of the labels and names you are inwardly and quietly, or outwardly and publicly, assigning to people you see, especially those who are in situations of need, suffering, pain, isolation. If possible, for a week or so make daily, even hourly lists of all the names you internally or externally give others. Try changing the names you ascribe to someone and see how it changes your perception of them.*

THE STORY OF NAMING AND MISNAMING

In the beginning, God named. Existence owes itself to God's naming. "Let there be light," said God, and there was light. What God named became reality. Naming causes being. This grand theological depiction in Genesis 1 permeates the Bible's vision of God. The faithfulness of God *(hesed)* means that what God says and what God does are one. The reliability between God's word and deed, between God's promise and action, forms the origin and potential for being human in speech as well as in action.

By contrast, the discordant story of human history as told in Scripture resounds with the perpetual breakdown between human word and deed. From the start our capacity for rightly naming included our freedom to misname. Such misnaming both reveals things that have changed and contributes to their changing fur-

ther. When "brother" became a mere label rather than a relationship of love, there was no longer a reason to be his keeper (Gen 4).
A tower in Babel held people's aspirations of making a name for
ourselves: one that was privileged, proud and overreaching (Gen
11). Misnaming misidentifies who we are, and who we are in relation to others. The consequences are everywhere.

The word of God to Abraham asserts that the hope of the world
hangs on a promise (Gen 12; 15). In this unique covenant-making
ceremony, participated in by the two promise-making parties to
the agreement, only God (symbolized by the smoking pot and the
flaming torch) bears the obligation of the promise to create, bless
and use a people. Hope is not in balance based on whether Abraham will keep any promises. The hope is that God will, that what
the Lord says and what the Lord does will be one.

God's promise to Abram, starting with a child, named a future
and created a hope ex nihilo (again) for a couple who were barren,
vulnerable and weak (Gen 12). Despite their laughter (whether in
faith or disbelief), despite their scheme to fulfill God's promise via
Hagar (whether in faith or disbelief), God was faithful. When
Abram passed the test of faith in the unity of God's word and deed,
God changed his name to Abraham. The absurd extremity of
God's later command to Abraham to sacrifice Isaac became a test
of how far Abraham would go in trusting the God who names and
does. The whole story of Israel thus emerges out of trusting the
faithful naming of God.

"Hearing their groaning" under the oppression of Egypt, God
remembered his promise and people (Ex 1–2). Their deliverance
from bondage and gift of liberation again turned on word and action, on God's naming himself and those God called his people.
"Yahweh" reveals God's name in promise: "I am the One who is
and who will be there for you" (Ex 3). Moses had a ministry only
insofar as he lived and served in the name of Yahweh. Israel's hope
in the midst of their slavery came from the God who rightly named

their suffering and need, and who asserted by promise a reality greater than their condition. "Let my people go," when spoken to Pharaoh by Moses under the authority of Yahweh, set the powerless free. Being properly named by God delivered Israel from any notion that their political, economic or physical circumstances meant they belonged to Pharaoh.

The reality God declared in naming them his own and in asserting their freedom trumped any other category or power that held them. Justice was done when by God's authority Egypt's misnaming of Israel was confronted and stopped. Yahweh's power swallowed the might of Pharaoh's troops. To bear Yahweh's name meant living Yahweh's way. To live under God's law was to be the way of enacting the character of God, of becoming those who live like the God who named them and whom they named. To live and walk God's way—Torah—was key to what God perpetually desired for Israel, and through Israel for the nations. This would be an indispensable part of how they would be "blessed to be a blessing" to the nations (Gen 12). By putting Yahweh's name first as God, all other acts of naming (including other possible deities, ourselves, our neighbors, our world) find their rightful place. All other words flow from this supreme speech-act. No rival to this Name exists.

Reflection. In ordinary life, our naming neglects, forgets and abuses God's way of naming. What are examples of that in your life this week? What happens or doesn't happen when you misname someone, that is, give them a name that they don't deserve and that diminishes them in your sight or in that of others? Are you aware of doing this? How aware are others around you? How aware are those you are misnaming?

DO WE HEAR OURSELVES?

Embedded in this practice of rightly naming God comes the ne-

cessity to name everyone and everything truthfully. The Ten Commandments can be read as a series of statements shaping our perception and engagement as human beings, reflecting life in God's
name and restraining Israel's temptation to misname God, other
gods, ourselves or our neighbor. They instruct Israel to avoid doing that by not overreaching in their own name. What, after all,
are covetousness and adultery, let alone murder, if not extending
one's name against that of someone else? Yahweh seeks a people
who reflect his name in how they speak and act in the world. The
Old Testament Law restrains Israel's power by putting it under
the greater power of Yahweh, the Lord of truth and justice, the
One the New Testament says is the giver of the perfect law of love
and liberty. By that Name a world properly and truly named is to
be re-created and, in humility, will bow to reflect that (Phil 2:5-
11). God, who sees the heart, eventually names David as Israel's
unlikely king. So David becomes king as one who mirrors this
divine naming, as "a man after [God's] own heart" (1 Sam 13:13-
14). The loss of this consistency, as evidenced in David's adulter-
ous relationship with Bathsheba, in his killing of Uriah and in his
failure to own his failure, becomes an element of the decay and
eventual dissolution of Israel that was warned by the prophets.

The first burden of the prophets is to name the sin of God's people: to tell them that the God they name by their profession of faith
and the One they name by their lives are contradictory. Unlike the
God they worship, Israel sells "the needy for a pair of sandals"
(Amos 2:6); they seek God "as if they were a nation that practiced
righteousness" (Is 58:2); they give themselves to sabbath festivals
that God "hates" (Is 1:14). As a consequence of these contradictions, they are actually misnaming God and lying to themselves
and others.

The second burden of the prophets then is to name the judgment of God on God's people as a consequence of their actions,
and also as a sign of hope. Misnaming is serious business and has

profound implications. The promises of God to make and bless a people do not erase accountability or judgment on those same people. In fact, they carry with them an accountability obligation precisely because the blessing is for the sake of recognizable transformation.

Humanity's contradictory nature was part of what God's covenant with Israel sought to reverse. When Israel's words and acts were as inconsistent as those of the alien and the stranger, Israel faced a crisis. This theme mounted to the point that Israel was sent into exile. They were given a new language, a new culture, a new pressure to assimilate, and in the midst of that, God was trying to teach them to speak and act in ways that honor Yahweh. They were to live in Babylon and show that they belonged to Yahweh. They were to seek the welfare of their enemies, and in doing so gain their own welfare (Jer 29). God disciplined Israel by intensifying the challenge rather than lightening it. Their exile was an additional measure of how much rightly naming matters to God.

Reflection. When you see others being misnamed, what is your internal response? Do you tend to identify with the misnamer or the misnamed? Why? What do you do about this if the person misnamed is present? is not present? Are the responses similar or different? How do you wish you would respond? What would it take for you to make that kind of response?

A New Name

John the Baptist starts his announcement of the coming of the kingdom of God by calling people to repent and be baptized (Mt 3). In other words, they are to name what's wrong and get cleansed in order to start living under a new name, the name of the One who comes and whose sandals John is unworthy to untie. This announcement of the kingdom presumes the need to name rightly who we are and who we are not, that is of first importance. Repentance is a naming in word and deed, not just one or the other. It's a turning from contradiction toward consistency, internal and external, human and divine, toward appearance and reality.

LIFE IN THE NAME

The Synoptic Gospels' birth narratives start with another announcement of God's perpetual gift: hope hangs (again and still) on an unlikely promise (Mt 1; Lk 1). The hope is that God's word and God's act will be the same. In this instance the renewal of a messianic promise will be fulfilled in the birth of a baby to be named Jesus, "for he will save his people from their sins" (Mt 1:21). The Gospel of John names this unity of God's supreme speech-act this way: "In the beginning was the Word, and the Word was with God, and the Word was God" (Jn 1:1). Jesus calls "anyone with ears to hear" to listen and follow him (Mk 4:9, 23). What he repels is hypocrisy of word and action, of religiosity without character, of law without grace, of form without substance, of name without reality, of judgment toward others without examining ourselves.

What he commands is a life that says and does the same things, and does them in the name he reveals and accepts as "Lord." It means renaming the ones some know as "sinners," "harlots," "tax collectors," "Gentile dogs," "drunkards," "lepers," "beggars," and addressing them with new names: "daughter," "sister," "friend," "disciple," "neighbor." This renaming changes and unnerves many of us. It is easier to "tithe mint, dill, and cummin, and . . . [neglect] the weightier matters of the law: justice and mercy and faith" (Mt 23:23). But then, it's clear throughout the Bible that rightly naming is anything but natural or easy. It requires that we become transformed namers, new people who draw from the taxonomy, the loving and just frame, by which we are all seen in the heart of God.

Actions, more than words, are the louder and more telling element in naming. So Matthew 25 tells us that those who actually feed, clothe and serve name their brother and sister rightly, as Jesus does, in contrast to those who don't see Jesus in those brothers or sisters, nor reflect the character and love he would wish them to express. Jesus said, "It is not what goes into a man, but what comes out" (Mt 15:11) that tells the most about who he is. For good and for ill, we inevitably reveal the name we follow and the kingdom we seek.

The gospel changes our name and our future. This means "there is therefore now no condemnation for those who are in Christ Jesus" (Rom 8:1). In other words, the life, death and resurrection of Jesus change the taxonomy by which God names us and therefore how we are to name God, ourselves and others. Jesus says, "I no longer call you servants. . . . Instead, I have called you friends" (Jn 15:15). "Chosen, . . . holy and beloved," says Paul (Col 3:12). The multiplying effect of this inward change in which all things are made new, in which we take every thought captive to Christ, in which we are transformed by the renewing of our minds out of true worship, leads to a new way of seeing, naming and living in the world.

Baptism is the sacrament of right naming, of being named by the love of God in the name of the Father and the Son and the Holy Spirit. In our identification with Christ's death and resurrection, we are named by grace for a new life. For those baptized as infants, this is done in anticipation of the child growing into the identity claimed for them long before they could ever do so for themselves. It emphasizes our dependency on God's initiating love. For those baptized as adult believers, baptism means accepting life in the name of the Father, the Son and the Holy Spirit by faith, which moves us from death to life. This sacrament places right naming at the very core of what God's work of justice and mercy does for the world. Life in this Name is meant to display and enact God's identification with us and ours with God. Seeing, naming and acting in this Name means giving away the life we've received because that is what Jesus himself displays and makes possible. It is not too much to say this book is simply an encouragement to live a baptized, rightly named life.

What we are made for and what the kingdom of God will produce is this: One day "every knee should bend, in heaven and on earth and under the earth, and every tongue should confess that Jesus Christ is Lord, to the glory of God the Father" (Phil 2:10-11). In that act, humanity and the whole cosmic order will be naming in word and deed that for which everyone and everything has been made.

Reflection. In what ways is this biblical theme of naming and renaming familiar to you? Is it part of how you think about your own life as a disciple? How do you experience being named or renamed by God? What does this theme of naming mean to you personally? to how you name others in your life? Why? How has your name been changed by the name of Jesus in your life?

TAXONOMY OF GOD'S HEART

Worship—the lifestyle of waking up to God, to the work of God in the world and to living that way—holds out hope that the love and justice of our hearts can come to mirror the love and justice of God's heart. The transformation of our hearts through lives of personal and public worship renews our capacity to name God, our neighbors and ourselves truly so that we might act justly. To live a life of worship, loving God with all our heart, mind, soul and strength, and loving our neighbor as ourselves, recalibrates how we live. Worshiping God can rewrite what's in our hearts with a message different from the one imprinted by our nurture and experience. Incrementally, through worship lived and practiced, we come to share the taxonomy of God's heart, seeing and feeling the love and justice of God.

What gives birth to this biblical vision of justice, to this process of renaming? The God who said, "'Let there be light'; and there was light" (Gen 1:3). "In the beginning was the Word, and the Word was with God, and the Word was God" (Jn 1:1). God created by naming: "Let there be light," and "Let us make humankind in our image" (Gen 1:26). The first job God gave humanity was to name the creatures. Naming is as primary to our being made in God's image as almost anything else we might, well . . . name. The ability to name carries with it our special capacity for relationship, including our potential for not just seeing but actually perceiving, acknowledging and affirming personal identity and worth. Love names us rightly. What need could be more primal to our daily experience of being human? In lives of worship we are meant to gain and practice the loving and just taxonomy of the heart of God. We practice reordering our perspectives in light of the truth and grace of Jesus Christ by whom everyone and everything is renamed.

We learn to name rightly God, our neighbor and ourselves. It's not about a new set of labels. It's about learning to live in the world as people who are named from the inside out by the God who made us, who is now remaking us and wanting us to be agents of that grace toward others. In a world of misnaming and misnamed people, a world where the injustices of name-calling undermine integrity, value, honor and the meaning of human lives, faithful worship is God's antidote to such distortion. God's heart teaches me to see the neighbor I call "fool" as "beloved." In the process, God's heart teaches me to confess my own distorted vision, my own dismissive relegation of my neighbors to a status they do not deserve. God's heart calls me to look again, to love, serve, forgive again.

Unchecked, however, our everyday naming of the people and the world around us gives life and takes it away—in small ways and in very large ones.

I can still feel the impact of a highly musical friend one day confidently calling me musical. No one had ever called me that. I didn't really play an instrument. I was no soloist. I didn't live with music constantly around me. Yet what made this comment so remarkable was that I instantly felt thoroughly known and loved. Why? Because I was being named in the way that touches my core. The musicality of my life, fundamental and invisible as it is, has to do with my soul—not with instruments. It's about my way of being in the world, not about notes being played. The sheer unexpected grace of being named "musical" by my friend stunned me because he got me. It's by no means the most important thing about me, but he got me in a way that noticed, validated and appreciated something that is deeply true about me even though it is usually missed. Being rightly named means being truly known. It changes our lives. If that's true about being named in small things, how much more is it true with respect to the things that really matter.

Embedded in our words and actions are the names we give to and receive from others. Gestures of value, nods of recognition, glances of curiosity, looks of compassion, signs of paying attention build one another up. Power can be measured by our capacity to give names that stick. Middle school teaches us this, if nothing

else. Every time the church gathers in worship, we gather as those
bearing names not our own: Inadequate. Failure. Bad Parent. Fat.
Through sins of omission and commission, through our own deliberate fault, we can be deluded or oppressed by the naming and
misnaming we experience and perpetrate. Suffering, individually
and collectively, intensifies when it's not named or is named
wrongly. Injustice wracks our world with the complex legacy of
God's treasured creatures misnaming God, misnaming ourselves
and misnaming our neighbor. It's our abuse of power and it's our
undoing. A lifestyle of worship is God's antidote.

Most years at an annual church leadership retreat I led, I would
introduce new elders to everyone present. I did not give a description of their activities or their work, but a more intimate and personal honoring of why I saw them as treasured gifts. When I first
did this and new elders came up in tears afterward expressing
what my comments had meant to them, it was clear that naming
matters more than I could have guessed. Over the years some have
said it was their personal highlight of being an elder. Naming can
give life.

Dalits ("Untouchables") in India are required by Hindu tradition to be given one name, and it must be derogatory: Ugly. Stupid.
Dung. Imagine the transformation when they discover that, in Jesus, God came as a Dalit (itself an extraordinary shock of rightly,
if unexpectedly, naming God), and that he has the power to rename them: Chosen. Holy. Beloved. "Behold, all things are new."
Indeed. As human beings and as Christ's disciples, ours is a vocation of naming. By God's grace, our calling is to live into our own
real names as we help others discover theirs. In turn, they can so
live and name the people and the world around them so that what
has been lost is found, and where they were blind they now see.
When we live this way, we are participating in doing justice, loving
kindness and walking humbly before our God (Mic 6:8). What else
is required by the One we name Lord? The problem is that out of

the heart of our misperception come the names that miss, dismiss, dishonor, distance and even destroy.

> **Reflection.** *Over these weeks, where are you seeing God's taxonomy of heart becoming more familiar to you and more fully your own? How is this happening? What spiritual practices are most helpful in nurturing this new heart? Where is your heart most responsive? most resistant to these changes? If paying more for fair-trade products cut into your budget, for example, would you (or do you already) make that choice?*

Social Naming

Lives are made and lost through naming. Every time we order the world around us we enter into the complex territory of naming. In other words, naming is one of the most common and profound expressions of human power in the world. Whatever our station in life and culture, society and influence, we all get to name "reality" as we see it. We get it right. We get it wrong. We get it both ways and all ways. We can't stop ourselves from naming. Whatever we believe, think and feel emerges from and then shapes who and how we name. Each time we name, whether in word or deed, we reveal our perception of what we think matters. What happens is a series of personal and systemic acts that unjustly misname people. Our power to name holds within it the possibility, in fact the probability, that we will also misname. The burden of this book is the injustice against misperceived people living misnamed lives in a misnamed world. The individual and collective injustice of misnaming is near the heart of our daily personal and global undoing.

THE JUSTICE AND INJUSTICE OF NAMING

Misnaming creates the verbal landscape that contributes to the rife injustice of our world. All of the "isms" are examples of the damage that naming contributes: racism, classism, sexism. Everywhere, people suffer the pain and loss that come from their abusers calling them by the wrong names: stupid, ugly, meaningless, chattel, one of "them," property, deserving of their pain. By such lies, misnaming helps foster an environment in which people and their circumstances are managed by an elaborate language game.

"Nike" trumps "sweatshops" in power all the time; the first is far more influential in shaping our behavior than the latter. When we read or hear about the twenty-eight million people who are slaves today, the most at any one time in all human history, the category "slave" is evocative, but still largely distant to many of the world's billions, including those who are reading this sentence. If we know some of the details of contemporary slavery, we no longer think of slave ships and plantations but of domestic workers, forced laborers and sex trafficking. To acknowledge that people are truly enslaved is much more accurate than if their situation were euphemized or unrecognized. It's an improvement over "the poor," of which the slaves are an invisible part. But this is nowhere near being the same as "my neighbor, the slave" or "my brother, the slave" or "my mother, the slave." The ordinary, prevalent injustice of misnaming can suddenly become exposed.

A serious foot injury put Susan, a friend of mine, in a wheelchair for several months. On the first day of being wheelchair-bound, she went to the Department of Motor Vehicles to get a handicapped tag for her car. As this blonde, attractive, articulate, Ph.D. scientist and educator was sitting in her wheelchair in line for a clerk, a man in front of her spoke to her. In an exceedingly exaggerated, slow, overenunciated way that some might use to talk to a mentally disabled child, he asked, "Would . . . you . . . like . . . to . . . go . . . in . . . front . . . of . . . me?" Susan rushed through various "naming questions" in her own mind: *Is he mentally impaired? Does he have a speech impediment? Is he emotionally unstable?* Then it dawned on her that he was responding to how he perceived her: this had to do with how he was naming her, not how she might name him, let alone herself. "I'm not in any hurry," she said in clear, easy diction. "After all, I'm the one sitting down." He seemed surprised and slightly confused since Susan was clearly so different from what he had presupposed. He had been naming her on the surface based on false stereotypes. This type of scene was repeated for Susan many times over the next several months. People would address those who happened to be standing near her wheelchair rather than her, as though she was deaf or mute as well as physically disabled. Clearly, the assumption was that she was not capable of interaction herself—that she was not who she is.

Unlike many, Susan can immediately explain and rightly name herself. But it takes little effort to imagine the crushing, possibly permanent injustice of being wrongly named, without the personal power to challenge, assert, redefine who you really are and therefore how you deserve to be known and treated. When a priceless, spirited little eight-year-old girl in Southeast Asia, for example, is sold into sex trafficking, she suffers the tragic injustice of being misnamed: she becomes a sexual commodity, a convenience, a "trick," a body, a plaything. Her literal name is changed. In the course of it all, she is functionally named "no one." As a result, if she thinks or feels, if she hurts or suffers, if she lives or dies, it doesn't matter. Within the misnaming is the brutality that attempts to expunge her as a human being. And even if her existence registers in the chart of the nearly one million other children sold into sex trafficking each year, her name is not really recovered. She may then be remembered as a data point, which can be better than "no one," but still a far cry from Seong Li, beloved child, "fearfully and wonderfully made."

> **Reflection.** *How have you experienced being wrongly named by someone in authority or power in your life? How did you feel? How did or does it affect you? Who is someone you have wrongly named? What do you think has been the impact of that for him or her? Is it possible for this to be changed?*

NAMING AND POWER

Naming is deeper than labeling. It includes the labels we give to things and people, but it is primarily a matter of the heart. Names are given in the heart and then embodied in words and actions. Names are first and foremost expressions of relationship. Embedded in our words and actions are the names we give to and receive from others. Gestures of value, nods of recognition, glances of curiosity, looks of compassion and signs of paying attention build up one another. Alternatively, when negative words and actions combine, naming can strip or even threaten a person's life.

As human beings we unavoidably name. Everywhere we go, we name. Everything we encounter, we name. Responding to the world around us means we will frame what we see in certain ways, and when we do so, we will be implicitly or explicitly naming whatever or whomever we encounter by attention, attitude, words, responses and actions. What happens when people in our world, individually and collectively, have no small army of faithful truth tellers from whom to hear and learn and practice their real names? What happens when people are alone, or worse, when they are trapped in systems or relationships through which their names are garbled, fractured, twisted or lost?

Our human capacity to name comes as a divine gift and vocation that reflects our being made in the image of God (Gen 1). Part of the human crisis, however, is that out of our hearts we misname our neighbors, ourselves and God. No one is spared the devastating consequences.

Everywhere injustice thrives, people are misnamed. Injustice occurs daily by simple and complex acts of misnaming. Injustice breeds in and spreads through these poisonous distortions. Naming attaches to our outside even as it makes claims about our inside. In most cases we simply assume that the names we give are the right ones, and they go deep enough to assign in our hearts the further implication of whether, therefore, that person is relevant or irrelevant to us, a threat or a tease, entertainment or a distraction. On and on the list goes. Our emotional intelligence and our moral visions will cause variation in this speedy and ubiquitous process. When we stop and consider things, most of us realize we don't know another's heart, we don't stand inside another's experience, we truly do not know or see another as they really are. But all the time we act as if we do. Although we don't know the whole story of a person or group of people, we blithely ascribe analysis, blame, responsibility, failure, disdain, worth.

Sticks and stones may break our bones, but words can tear our heart out. On the personal, social and global scale, naming occurs with relentless power. By our names we are defined and shaped, for good and for bad, with justice and injustice. By naming we grant and take away life. Yet most days and most times, this is so imbedded in the rhythm of life that we have little awareness of what is happening and its potency. Everywhere injustice is found, misnaming contributes to and sustains the lie, the destruction.

What is needed to change this is more than improved labeling. Naming is a matter of the heart; it happens everywhere all the time.

Reflection. *Recall one of the most significant experiences of misnaming in your life or that of someone else (known to you personally or whom you have known of in some way). What happened? What was the impact? Why? How do you feel about that experience? What does it lead you to conclude about the power of misnaming?*

A FLAIR

It took less than five seconds for the young man who came into the coffee shop that afternoon to start being named. It had been a fairly quiet place and then, with flair and a flurry, with long, dyed-black hair—the front third of which was bleached very blond—and wearing jeans, a decorated white down vest and flip-flops, and carrying a red-and-white-striped fabric shoulder bag, he strode to the counter to ask the baristas in a loud and exaggerated voice if they were accepting applications.

"Hey, you guys, I am here!" he grinningly announced as he raised and lowered his palms several times on the countertop. "So, I really need a job," he sang. "Can I work here? I really have lots of bills and I need to make some money. I suppose I could sell my body, but maybe I should sell coffee instead. This is a coffee place, right? Ooo, I like your earrings," he said, holding up his fingers in front of his pursed lips for a moment before he went on. "So, what do you think? I don't really like coffee. But they said next door at the pizza place that it would take a really, really long time to get a job there, so I decided to come over here."

"Well," the junior manager said, "we want people to work here who like what we sell." In a few more minutes, after some kind words of discouragement from the barista, referring him to some other place nearby, he was off, loudly announcing into the air that he was, in any case, "sooo excited."

There is not a chance he goes unnamed by those he meets. Is the primary impetus in his story his own self-naming that he enacts, or is he performing names others have given him? He is clearly aware of a public of some sort, and has the need or desire to play to them. An inelegant dandy would be one way of naming or describing him. A cultivated flair and style of speech and dress meant to leave an impression. And he does. Out of his heart come all kinds of signs of distinction, need, hunger, confidence, insecurity, longing.

Out of the hearts of those in the café, in the conservative as well as hippie mountains near Santa Cruz, south of San Francisco, came names of various kinds no doubt. I looked around, all the people in the café had at least turned their attention in his direction, and presumably had sized him up and assigned some inner name to what was unfolding before them. It would not be difficult to imagine a wide range of epithets that might be assigned to him, and with each would come some corresponding sense of assessment, evaluation, humor, disdain, regard or disgust. The treatment this young man receives in the world is affected by his sense of self, which is both publicly framed and self-imposed. Whatever the issues of his inner life, they would seem to be of a piece with his outer life. The lens by which he sees is a projected image. What is fed back to him are similar images confirming that he sees truly, yet so much that is important about him is not visible and seems inaccessible.

His sense of treatment in the world might seem entirely just (he gets what he expects and asks for in affection and rejection), but it might also seem entirely like an unjust charade and the tale of a truly unknown, unseen victim.

Reflection. Notice today the social naming going on around you in various settings. What were some of the names? What caused them to be assigned? How fair or unfair is that to any of the individuals involved? Have you ever been socially misnamed in a way that caused a crisis for you? Why? What was it? How did you respond?

COOL GUY

He was ahead of me at the crosswalk by about forty feet, going the same direction I was. What first caught my attention was the narrowness of his neck and the stiff-lined tendons that disappeared down the back of his well-ironed shirt. His back seemed like an empty space, draped with shirt fabric. The belt on the tan slacks he wore seemed to gather up extra material in his trousers, giving the impression that his pants were dangling on the line, exaggerating his thin waist. He had the intentional, even trendy style of other mid-twenties urbanites.

The crosswalk light changed and he stepped out toward the other side of the street. With his first lunge it was now evident that his left foot and ankle turned in dramatically toward the right, and that this thin, well-dressed, pleasant-looking young man was affected by some degree of what seemed to be cerebral palsy. The erect calm and coolness he exuded when he was waiting for the light suddenly became a jerking, leaning exertion. As I came even with him in the crosswalk, I noticed two things: first, his facial stubble, meticulously and fashionably groomed just below his jaw line; and second, a small interior smile. Once on the other side of the street, I broke away to the left while he continued straight ahead. In my heart I winced as I replayed the cumulative impact of this young man's groomed appearance colliding with the broader social messaging of his cerebral palsy. He was clearly presenting himself as attentive, engaged and understatedly cool. It seemed a statement of understandable and deserved hope.

This impression wobbled the moment he moved. It wobbled enough in my heart and mind for me to feel that the currency of life he was offering would be hard for him to exchange. He struck me as one who clearly exerted control of his life in his demeanor, appearance and purposefulness. His fashion choices suggested he fit within a good mix of people his age. He would probably be missed, dismissed, in the sea of others who are more able-bodied. He clearly carried the subculture of his generation and moment, but his wobbliness seemed more likely to define him.

His dissimilarity from others would shape his life more than his similarity. Does he know and see this in the way it appears from outside or is it quite different in ways I and others cannot see or know? Does he name himself as others do? Does he know how unjustly he is seen and named? Is his an act of defiance against that injustice or despite it? Are these reflections on my part their own act of misperception and misnaming? How might my assumptions distort who he is and how he lives in the world?

> **Reflection.** *Think of someone you know, observe or know about whose external name is not their internal one. Why is there this difference? Why and how does it matter? How do you respond to the dissonance between the two?*

LINGUISTIC MANAGEMENT

Naming can be socially sanitizing with the forehand and unjust on the backhand. Naming can take the bare, twitching nerve-endings of life and cast them in ways so as to sanitize that raw material. It is our tendency toward euphemism, toward disinfecting human need with words that make it seem so different from and so much less than it actually is. It happens through categorization, for example. When we classify people as "the poor," we use a verbal convention for generalization that cleanses the particularities of actually being poor. "The poor," after all, could be used to designate everyone from the top of the American poverty level to the utterly destitute in Africa or Asia. To have shabby housing, a poor diet and inadequate medical care is, however, different from literally having nothing—including access to clean water. So the category does not adequately convey the actual experience of being poor, though it claims to apply in ways that do. Being poor in America can mean a five-figure income, which is not what being poor in India and Africa connotes.

In other words, it is possible that such naming can designate a demographic standard (e.g., annual income, health statistics, access to education, etc.), but when used to refer to people, not just statistics, the name sanitizes out the soul-numbing tedium of waiting in long lines for bureaucratic action, the labor of walking miles to get water, the smell of poverty and disease, the sight and discomfort of bloated stomachs, the stench of no sanitation, the sorrow of a parent who has no money for school fees, the resignation that comes with the offer of free antiretroviral drugs for HIV treatment without the means to get basic food, without which those life-giving drugs become lethal.

Or take the name "prisoner." Again, it is a single word for an extraordinary array of experiences that is blurred and sanitized when a general designation frames what is a personal and individual experience. The prisoner's age and psychological condition make for the first variation. Then there is the alleged wrong that has brought on the imprisonment. Tens of thousands of prisoners around the world have never had charges brought against them. Then the issue arises of whether there is any general rule of law in the country in question and whether it has served in any way to seek justice for others in similar circumstances. There is the prison itself, the density of prisoners, the nature of their varying crimes, the presence or absence of sanitation, the amount of physical or sexual abuse that occurs within that facility. All these disinfecting acts of naming are part of *us* living in a world radically different from *them*.

"Middle class" names not being "rich" and not being "poor." Naming becomes a filtering system that screens in and screens out, without accuracy and sometimes without empathy. It's about linguistic management that is much easier to handle with distance and disconnection.

They is one of our most powerful verbal disinfectants. *We* exclude ourselves. *They* are other and distinct, and usually less than we are. *We* feel sure the demarcations that divide are real, legitimate, defensible, clear. Our assumption is that *we* don't want to be one of *them*, and such a verbal designation underlies and to some degree assures us of the fact that we won't be.

Reflection. What euphemisms do you notice yourself using when you know or acknowledge underneath a darker name for someone you dislike, disdain, judge? From where do those perceptions and names come? To what sorts of traits or actions in someone else are they most likely to attach? Do you believe they are justified? What would the other person say in response?

Distorted Names

Always together, always friends; that's the way they had been since preschool. Butter and Cream, people called them, though the two did not fully know why or what was meant by it. Until, that is, a new girl in their third-grade class wanted to make a friend and wanted it to be Cream but not Butter. The new girl pulled and cajoled, tattled and whispered, to draw and quarter that long friendship. One day, this interloper spit a new name at Butter, "Chink." Butter took the verbal blow and, through tears, held her stomach, and kicked the new girl, who never got her friendship with Cream. In fact, Cream told the girl she was mean, though she had to ask later what *Chink* meant. Although through this experience Cream came to love Butter even more, she could never see Butter quite the same.

BUTTER AND CREAM

The two girls' blind innocence had seen no difference between them, but this incident inserted a filter. Though small, a distance between them was noticeable where none had been. Cream and Butter became their private nicknames as their given names of Lucy and Min became more prominent once they were older. The two-peas-in-a-pod life they had known became more and more like two peas in two pods, albeit still close together. By the time they reached middle school, they were more independent, not always together, but still best friends. They were each other's default friendship when the swings of other relationships passed through the emotional battleground of teenage highs and lows. They knew each other in ways no one else did, and that mostly meant safety and joy.

High school brought some changes. It started in their sophomore year when they both admitted having a crush on the same boy, Simon. He was Taiwanese, and had been born and lived there until he entered high school. Lucy and Min had barely noticed him last year, but over the summer things had changed. As school started, he was different: taller, more relaxed, funny and very cute. It was Lucy who got his attention. To Min, this was not just disappointing, it was racist. She felt the sting of Simon's interest in "a cute white girl" and the rebuff of feeling excluded by someone of her own racial background. She felt betrayed by Lucy and rejected by Simon. She began to withdraw from her activities and friendships, and to lose herself in her school work. Min began to feel more and more alone as Simon and Lucy got closer. Seeing Lucy and Simon together every day drove Min to get angrier and angrier. Lucy knew that Min was upset, but when Lucy tried to talk about it, Min refused. Upset herself, Lucy decided she would try to force Min to talk. One day after school, Lucy saw Min walking by herself and ran to catch up with her. Things were awkward and silent. Lucy blurted out in frustration, "Is this all about 'the Chink thing'?"

That did it. The friendship was over for Min. That breakdown would be talked about only when they saw each at their tenth reunion.

Reflection. Do you have any close friendships with people of a race or class other than your own? Can you think of a relationship you have had in which the racial and class distinction between you and the other person suddenly became an issue between you? How did it happen? Why? How did it affect each of you? How did you rename yourself or each other?

DISABLED HEARTS

Although it was decades ago, Frank remembers the day and the moment. He, his dad and his brother were playing with a football in the basement. The ball was not round, not easily handled by his four-year-old fingers. A wobble, the ball escaped, something crashed. A harsh word. In moments the ball, the dad and the older brother were outside. The four-year-old gazed up and out through the latticed windows to see the ball and the other two continuing their play on the back lawn. Left behind, he watched and knew as deeply as he had known anything that he was not *them*, nor were *they* him. He was not part of their *us*. "Not wanted" was his inner, now dominating name. Today reveals decades of implications. It's still not easy for this man to see beyond that childhood wound and the insecurity and fear of rejection that festers within it. Getting caught in a feedback loop of self-interest and protection is instinctive for him, even when it is counterproductive. He is locked in the small, sometimes silly, myopic prison of self.

That personal, interior drama portrays the vulnerability of the heart and the power of being wrongly named. Human beings are dust: easily scattered, blown away. The distortion in our heart's lifelong capacity to see ourselves and others can be the consequence of incidental moments, like a time in the basement with a ball. Pain leads to a confusion that leads to a lie that leads to damaged vision that leads to a failure to perceive with an unfearful heart. This is when the story goes fairly well, all things considered. This is not where the heart has been beaten, sat upon or pierced. This is only the heart roughed up a little. A heart that has been mauled or neglected or cut is going to face much greater challenges in seeing truly and engaging sacrificially.

Wounded, disabled hearts—the only kind there are—are the same hearts called to seek and do justice. It is like saying to someone who is sick, "Act well." That can happen, and does, but it is not easy or common. It can require decisions to juggle your own heartache in order to attend to someone else's. Perhaps as in the Special Olympics, courage and determination have to exceed the lack of some capacity. Only a few are willing and able to try.

Reflection. What, if any, painful memories of being misnamed have you experienced in your life or seen in the lives of others that prohibit you from being who you are? from using your gifts? from expressing your freedom? What has been the impact? What does it take to reverse the damage and to set the name right?

HARAMI

Mariam was five years old the first time she heard the word *harami*. It happened on a Thursday. It must have, because Mariam remembered that she had been restless and preoccupied that day, the way she was only on Thursdays, the day when Jalil visited her at the *kolba*. To pass the time until the moment that she would see him at last, crossing the knee-high grass in the clearing and waving, Mariam had climbed a chair and taken down her mother's Chinese tea set. The tea set was the sole relic that Mariam's mother, Nana, had of her own mother, who died when Nana was two. Nana cherished each blue-and-white porcelain piece, the graceful curve of the pot's spout, the hand-painted finches and chrysanthemums, the dragon on the sugar bowl, meant to ward off evil. It was this last piece that slipped from Mariam's fingers that fell to the wooden floorboards of the *kolba* and shattered. When Nana saw the bowl, her face flushed red and her upper lip shivered, and her eyes, both the lazy one and the good, settled on Mariam in a flat, unblinking way. Nana looked so mad that Mariam feared the jinn would enter her mother's body again. But the jinn didn't come, not that time. Instead, Nana grabbed Mariam by the wrists, pulled her close, and, through gritted teeth, said, "You are a clumsy little *harami*. This is my reward for everything I've endured. An heirloom-breaking, clumsy little *harami*." At the time, Mariam did not understand. She did not know what this word *harami*—bastard—meant. Nor was she old enough to appreciate the injustice, to see that it is the creators of the *harami* who are culpable, not the *harami*, whose only sin is being born. Mariam did surmise, by the way Nana said the word, that it was an ugly, loathsome thing to be a *harami*, like an insect, like the scurrying cockroaches Nana was always cursing and sweeping out of the *kolba*.[1]

In this opening to *A Thousand Splendid Suns*, Khaled Hosseini captures the profound force of an assigned and distorting name. Nana ascribes it to Mariam in bitterness and hatred, out of personal, social and religious brutality and rejection of Nana's own life. *Harami* is anything but incidental, fair or deserved. It holds for Nana a frame by which to contain and punish Mariam for what she was not responsible for and for what she cannot change. Nana had herself, of course, been tragically and unjustly named. The suffering and victimization of being (apparently) loved, and then rejected and banished to this remote *kolba* (very simple home), was Nana's bitter daily fruit. It had preceded and shaped everything about the way Nana passed along the distortion and abuse to Mariam, and it would in the end be the source of Nana's ultimate demise. The injury and poison in our hearts leak, affecting everyone and in the most ordinary ways making injustice a matter of the heart.

---

[1]Khaled Hosseini, *A Thousand Splendid Suns* (New York: Riverhead, 2007), pp. 3-4.

Reflection. Stigma can be excruciating. What stigmas, if any, have you ever been assigned or assigned to others with no choice of your own or of theirs? What are the most distressing ones you have experienced or witnessed (e.g., gender, race, intelligence, physical disability, class, skill, etc.)? What stigmas do you hear relegating people to neglect most readily and easily? Why?

Changing Names

A friend who was born in India
as a part of the Dalit caste was able, through the privilege and opportunity of education, to leave India and make a life for himself
that was largely free of the curse of his caste. (Names in the caste
system of India virtually establish whether you are human or not,
at least if your name is Dalit.) After several decades, he returned to
India and went back to visit his village and his two closest childhood friends, also Dalits. (The nature of this naming prison would,
of course, make it inappropriate and impossible to have close
friendships with children of other castes.) By the time these men
remet, they were all in mid-life. The two friends who had remained
in India had managed to position themselves through forms of cultural hiding so that they were no longer known as Dalits, nor did
they think of themselves as Dalit. In other words, each in their
own form of lying had left the limiting and distorting label that
was theirs by birth.

They had renamed themselves, in fact or in form, in order to
find freedom. Meanwhile, my friend had returned to India to reclaim his identity as a Dalit and was anxious to talk about this
with his boyhood friends. One of the more profound parts of their
reunion, however, was that these friends were now so entrenched
in their new names that when my friend began talking to them
about the three of them being Dalit, they would not admit to him
that they were Dalit. The power of names to define their lives had

now so renamed them that they could no longer recognize or admit, even to their close childhood friend, what their caste designation had been. The fear of acknowledging what he was saying and the price that could be paid as a consequence were enormous.

When you marry under the presumption that you are a higher caste than you are, especially if you are a Dalit, it means that everything, including life itself, could be at risk if your deception should become known. It would be tantamount to doing the unthinkable. Those were the circumstances of my friend's childhood pals. Their lives claimed the truth and freedom of their genuine human dignity and gifts, but doing so required that they culturally lie, that they embrace a cultural deception that had to be sustained or they could risk losing their families or even their lives.

Being named a Dalit is a life sentence that places nearly 180 million people off the bottom of the caste system into a subhuman category of existence.

That is a measure of just how unthinkable naming can be.

> **Reflection.** *You are probably not a Dalit, yet you live in a world of Dalits of many kinds, and we do little to change that reality. We live in a world of daily gender, racial, class and physical injustice perpetrated all around us. What signs of these patterns are you seeing this week? How do they help make people targets? How and why are they so easily doled out toward others?*

A CONTAGION OF THE HEART

In order to "bury the N-word," the National Association for the Advancement of Colored People (NAACP) conducted a memorial service, complete with pine box and flowers, during their July 2007 meeting in Detroit. The NAACP leaders are not alone in their concern over the increasing use of the N-word, not least in hip-hop lyrics and in African American street culture generally.

"It's a word with about as much bad history attached to it as any word I can imagine," said Jerry Herron, a professor of American studies at Wayne State University. Herron believes that the word is still so powerful because of the disturbing connections it has with the past as well as in the present. The potency of the N-word continues, he says, because "it refers to things that are woven into the fabric of our society that we haven't yet fixed. . . . I think if those things had been fixed someplace in the past, the N-word would be a lot less powerful than it is. But it refers not only to a bad history, but a bad present."[1]

Of course, there is no sense among NAACP leadership that a ceremonial rite will end the use of the N-word or neutralize its toxicity. Although its usage among whites may have greatly diminished over recent decades in the United States, according to the NAACP, the N-word is as common or even more ferocious among African Americans as it has ever been. The N-word is a complex identity marker for a whole ethnic group, for a culture and subculture, and for an individual as well. It's a name that hooks people to a past that still plays in the present. It has evocative currency. In hip-hop lyrics or street-talk, the N-word can feel self-referentially liberating to many African Americans who spew it with their perplexing combination of pride and anger, even as it symbolizes a kind of prison. It is a hate-filled name, but if society had changed, the word may have been neutralized of any contemporary power. It is not just a historic term of abuse but a living one; the venom attached to it still catapults the emotions and denigration into hearts. So, the NAACP instinctively and passionately wants to bury the word, but they are doing the very thing that they realize they cannot do: bury the N-word. Here is how one blogger expressed this sentiment at the time of this burial event:

---

[1] Jonnelle Marte and Andy Henion, "Banished: Thousands Say 'Good Riddance' to N-Word," *Detroit News,* July 10, 2007.

I am sorry to say that a ceremony burying the "N" word will not change racism in Detroit nor America. Racism is taught by parents and is passed on from generation to generation. Just as you acquire your parents' genes you learn their ignorance, and lack of compassion. Burying the "N" word is no different than placing "In God we Trust" on government and public buildings. Until we act like a country and a nation under God, words mean nothing and it is our actions for which we will be judged upon on earth and in heaven. This is why many countries do not trust the United States, we preach bringing democracy and freedom to Iraq, but allow our companies to profit from Communism, oppression, torture, and executions in China as long as we have cheap products. Is this the God we entrust?[2]

When it comes to naming, the blogger is right. It's deeper than labeling, and it cannot be changed at the surface. Naming is an act of the heart. It's an attribution of our core perception onto the people and things around us. Naming is what people do, not just what words do. Labels are hard enough to change. Names are something quite different.

> **Reflection.** *Why are names like the N-word so hard to bury? What "N-words" have you had used against you? What makes a word like that degrading? Have you tried or should you try to bury it? Why? What has happened in that effort? What (internally or externally) prompts you to use it or others to use it toward you?*

---

[2]Blog response by Andrew T. Linko, Brownstown, Michigan, to the Associated Press article by Joel Roberts, "Burying the N-Word," July 9, 2007.

VIRAL

Misnaming is viral, an invisible infection. Passed along without particular will or intent, names do their quite (and quietly) destructive work all the same. No dictionary teaches us the N-word, or some equivalent; we just feel it from the moment it first rings in our bodies. Part of its power is that it gets us by the heart. It specifically doesn't have to be explained or defined, and in some ways it defies attempts to do so. When we want to express feelings or attitudes, that viral infection hands us easy tools. It resides in us, often latently, leaving us with the impression that we are virus free of racism, for example, until with surprising stealth and speed and specificity, it shows itself in attitude or speech.

I am appalled to confess that my own insidious racism is most likely to appear in little moments of irritation and frustration, not in larger, more consequential encounters. I get cut off in traffic, someone in public acts in too loud or too passive a way, a parent disciplines their child in what seems to me like an overly aggressive way—those are the small moments when I can sometimes see that my internal reactions can be racially prejudiced. When I am honest with myself, it's in those moments that I attribute to someone's race a judgment based on individual style or attitude; I universalize the instance or particularize from the universal. While I believe that this has become less common in my life, I am aware in my spirit how the viral quality of misnaming is present in my life. Namecalling works this way, whether about race, body characteristics, personality, class, culture, ability, style or whatever else. Rumors and gossip are specific forms of this, but cultural practices can pass along the poison that includes and excludes, that values and devalues, that assembles people in relationships of privilege and disadvantage. Sometimes we inflict the virus on ourselves, or we internalize what we think we are being given by society.

Eating disorders can be an example of this pattern. The bias toward thinness idolized in our culture becomes a burden that perverts how a young woman (typically) sees her already thin body so that she sees it as obese, fostering a downward spiral that turns in on herself and jeopardizes her life. Achieving self-perceived thinness is an exquisitely neurotic standard—the perfect impossibility. It's a form of viral naming, an infection that often eludes the most concentrated professional intervention. This makes the experience of a friend of mine all the more fascinating for related but contrasting reasons.

My friend is a strong woman, powerful in her sense of herself and her dignity. After a lifetime of being seen as round, plump, heavy and fat and having tried to lose weight, she became a committed part of what she called affectionately the "Nazi version of Overeaters Anonymous." Astonishingly, she lost all the weight she needed to be height- and weight-proportional for a shorter woman. It was truly a remarkable transformation, paced over time, and an encouragement and joyful delight to herself and to her friends and community. The problem was that she got what she wanted. She lost the weight and became the size she wanted. She was now being named the way she had always named herself and wanted to be named by others. She looked like the inner self she had always seen. As that happened externally, however, she came to feel misnamed because now she was regarded for her body just as she had been disregarded for her body. And she wanted neither. The viral infection was there whatever she weighed. Now she has regained most of the weight she lost, because the virus lives on, both inside and all around her.

The viral impact of such misnamed naming compounds uncontrollably. It's the prejudiced air we breathe in and out every day, so much so that we don't even know it. It's affected by the winds of popular culture, by all forms of media, by our particular subculture, by our family of origin, by all the internal and external voices that shape how we see and engage the world around us.

As the perceiving, engaging, reflective, relational, meaning-making, linguistic creatures we are, naming is primal for us. What it's not is neutral. What it's not is containable. It can give life. It can take it away. What naming does endlessly and profoundly is affect every life every day.

> **Reflection.** What comes to you as an example of some viral name you have received or passed along that keeps you or others at the social margins where injustice is tolerated by those in power? How did or does that name spread? What does that tell you about its power and force? its attraction and utility?

PRESIDENT OBAMA

The first African American president of the United States. That combination of words is brand new. This racial category named alongside this role has never occurred before this presidency. It was a plausibility structure that had never been tried and even now, early in his presidency, the reality can hardly be imagined. For many older African Americans, President Barack Obama names what their dreams could hardly contain. They could not conceive of their nation in this way. This frame on the election of Barack Obama presents a new way of seeing our nation and, for many of its citizens, a new way of seeing themselves. It took two years of intense, bitter debate; an international economic recession; and unprecedented political cost and drama to make it possible for "African American" and "president of the United States" to become names that belong together. In fact, it took centuries.

The morning after the election, I was in a coffee shop filled with a mix of races. I watched a table of white, stay-at-home moms cry together with joy over Obama's election. I watched a young Asian businessman get tears in his eyes while talking to a friend he had celebrated with last night; sleep-deprived and still celebrating, he was elated and buoyant, and kept saying over and over, "I can't believe it." This was not just another election or another postelection day. It was a renaming of life in America.

Whatever a person's political views may be or whatever they have become during his time in office, the election of Obama was a renaming of America in the world. Given the global disdain that grew during the Bush era, in which the United States had been re-labeled from "land of opportunity" to "empire of aggression," from "nation of hope" to "land of fear," Obama's election is transformative. To some this is a moment in which the United States appears to be recovering its noblest vision and its shining past. What many around the world felt had disappeared now seems to be back, and back with an even more determined will to live and be different. America is not just a place with opportunity but a place of realized opportunity. All of this now names at a high cultural level the drama of events that has taken place because of access to money, power, communication and charisma, and the fate of a particular person at a particular time.

The trickle-down impact of this, being so joyfully claimed and anticipated, is still just unfolding. It will be a spotty, even disappointing, story going forward. It will not automatically yield a society free of racial prejudice and hatred. Less dramatically, you only needed to listen to the coverage of the election to hear the racist anger and disdain that was proclaimed by some of Obama's opponents.

A recent longitudinal study of race is even more striking. What it shows is that negative changes in social circumstances (e.g., poverty or jail time) "made people more likely to be perceived by interviewers as black and less likely to be seen as white." As one of the study's authors, Andrew Penner, says, "Race isn't a characteristic that's fixed at birth. . . . We're perceived a certain way and identify a certain way depending on widely held stereotypes about how people believe we should behave."[3] Obama's election is historic.

[3]K. Kaplan, "Study Details the Power of Negative Racial Stereotypes," *Los Angeles Times*, December 9, 2008.

Perhaps what has changed is that the plausibility of racial prejudice in quiet and sustained expression is no longer as infectiously viable. This election has created social and political leverage to tilt relationships and institutions toward racial justice and away from racial prejudice.

> *Reflection.* How do words shape what is socially or politically possible for our lives? How do they shape what is possible for the poorest of the world? What does "President Obama" represent as a change in name? What is or is not the impact of that change (if any)? What name might you seek to give to someone to help them live with freedom and dignity, justice and honor?

PASSIVE-AGGRESSIVE

Naming can be passive-aggressive, which is "the expression of negative feelings, resentment and aggression in unassertive ways." Naming is one of our most common ways of being passive-aggressive toward people, events and things.

Samantha Power's Pulitzer Prize–winning book, *"A Problem from Hell": America and the Age of Genocide*, traces the extraordinary history of the creation and establishment of the word *genocide*, as well as the twentieth-century history of the evil it names. Raphael Lemkin invented the word to try to capture in one term the decimating horror by which one group seeks to expunge another group. His hope was that the word would evoke moral repugnancy and compel the moral intervention demanded by such destruction. In 1948, after protracted and intense debate following the Armenian and Jewish Holocausts, the United Nations adopted the Convention on the Prevention and Punishment of the Crime of Genocide that settled on the following definition for the term:

Any of the following acts committed with intent to destroy,

in whole or in part, a national, ethical, racial, or religious group, as such:

> killing members of the group; causing serious bodily or mental harm to members of the group; deliberately inflicting on the group the conditions of life calculated to bring about its physical destruction in whole or in part; imposing measures intended to prevent births within the group; forcibly transferring children of the group to another group.[4]

The passage of this Convention was hard-fought. The history of its use has been passive-aggressive. The premise was that it would be the standard by which heinous acts would be consistently named, with the necessary inference that such designation would mean that the international community would then do all it possibly could to stop genocide wherever and whenever it occurred. Since 1948, however, we have seen genocides debated and conceded in Cambodia, Iraq, Bosnia, Rwanda, Congo and Darfur. Each time passionate debate precedes such naming, since the designation is so serious and consequential. In the passive-aggressive nature of naming, even having the evidence and the designation has not led to consistent international intervention. Political, economic or social passivity kicks in and the genocide continues. The debates clearly indicate that this designation carries such significance that being sure of the horrors is critical to the use of the word and the consequent moral actions that it would imply for the international community. But when the standard has been met and the horror classified, it is still possible to collapse it into passive vagueness. The word is given and taken away.

The structures we have empowered to act aggressively—by pronouncing *genocide* upon the necessary evidence—are invested with equivalent power to undercut international response through

[4]Samantha Power, *"A Problem from Hell": America and the Age of Genocide* (New York: Harper Perennial, 2002), p. 57.

passive inaction. The moral argument asserts that if it is clear that genocide is occurring, then the international community will respond with equally clear moral opposition by marshaling every necessary attempt to stop it. The excruciating irony is that we passively undermine that moral imperative through equivocating with the language of response. When we backpedal through passive-aggressive mumbling, we leave thousands, if not millions, functionally misnamed. The true name *genocide*, hard-fought for and justified, is reduced to a mere label. Naming and misnaming become a matter of life and death.

We turn names into labels when the situation (political or personal) demands it. We hold onto names with passion and commitment until they are challenged or grow too costly, at which point we let them go, presuming we can withdraw or qualify them. But they leave greater suffering in their wake.

We want words to mean something—most of the time. But the complexity of communication is that we want words to mean only what we *want* them to mean, as and when we want them to mean it—to convey what we feel or intend without the consequences of the choices we make. We want the power to pronounce names without incurring accountability for their implications.

Reflection. How do you feel about this history of the word genocide? *Why? Does any other example come to mind in a parallel vein? Does this breed cynicism, resignation or some other response for you? Why? How would you feel about this if you were someone in Darfur or Croatia or if your ancestors were Armenian?*

REALITY-CREATING

We are verbal creatures. We are given the language of words as one of our most powerful means of self-expression; we define reality around us in verbal categories and designations. One of the most magical parts of being a parent has been watching our children grow from nonverbal newborns to highly verbal children, youth and young adults. Helping children learn to name their inner and outer worlds is daunting, yet in the values of American middle-class life, a parent is instinctively aware that verbal skills have the power to fashion and affect a world. This can be illustrated in various ways, some more virulent than others. It seemed alarming and more than a little suggestive when the first word I heard from our older son was *more*. There's a reality-creating word. But some of the most powerful words have been later ones: *love, frustration, sadness, anger, hope, inquiry, reflection, passions*. His world has grown ever more complex both because of words, and as reflected in words.

We continue to learn as a family about words: when and how to speak, when to remain silent or to say less rather than more. Words can set off explosions, and they can quell worries or nerves. Words spoken can get us in trouble, but words unspoken can do so too. Knowing the difference is part of the process of growth. Some in our family love to talk, and some in our family are quieter. What we hold in common is the instinct and the need to name one another and our world. As children grow up, they first use the language and categories that come from the adults or possibly from older siblings in their lives. Gradually, other influences from books, media, music, school and culture shape the stockpile of words that we come to apply as we live each day. What we don't know, don't suspect and often never realize is that none of this is neutral. All of it is affected by the contexts we live in. We use language to make and define the world. This is not in the sense that we fabricate people, places and things by our words—but in some ways we almost do.

Consider, for example, the influence (though diminishing to a degree) that speech and accent can have in defining your life and its possibilities in some places in Britain. The class system in Britain is breaking down and being changed in many ways, principally because of economic growth, immigration and education. I once spent a week as a patient in a hospital in Cambridge. To while away the time in my recovery, I would close my eyes and try to guess, on the basis of various accents I would hear, which job that person was doing in the room. The more refined the accent a person had, the higher the professional stature. The broader the accent, the lower the job in the hospital pecking order. Hearing a Cockney accent from a senior physician would be highly unlikely. In fact, it would be reality-creating by being reality-changing.

> **Reflection.** *How do you find yourself or others creating reality by the words you assign to others or to circumstances? How do you do that? Why? In what ways are you using words that imprison others? distance others? set others free? Is this just? How has your life been created for better and worse by the names others have given you? How could you practice naming others redemptively?*

TRUE NAMING

One of the most profound marks of justice is the naming of the truth about the victim, the injustice, the perpetrator, the law, the consequences. Of course, discerning the right names about such things can be difficult. But more often the only real difficulty is the lack of will and resources to do so. Power is on the side of the misnamers.

David, the young man in Nairobi arrested, maimed and imprisoned on false charges (see chap. three), had people with power saying who David was and what he had done. They were lies, but David was without a voice. He was held under an unnamed, false, capital offense he was not guilty of. He had no control of when or why or how his case would proceed. He would be tried in a language he did not know and, if convicted, he would be killed. At the last moment David was appropriately represented in court by the

International Justice Mission and was eventually released. The corrupt police were jailed because of their unjust abuse. True names attached to the right people meant true justice.

When the brick kiln owner in India is finally named as the enslaving, abusive, illegal perpetrator he is, light shines in the darkness. Human value demands human accountability. The one who abused the power to name is now named by the law and its judiciary. This is justice, and it is good news.

When the powerless AIDS widow hears the judge pronounce that her house is being restored to her and her children after it had been grabbed by the extended family, justice has renamed her. The weight of the law has stood with her, blessed her and restored to her the means of life for today and for tomorrow. This is justice, and it is good news.

When the little girl is rescued from the Asian brothel and given aftercare and schooling, and her captors are tried and sentenced, she really understands that her name has gone from "no one" to "treasure." This is justice, and it is good news.

Justice renames the forgotten as the remembered, the widow as the loved and the oppressed as the treasured. Naming gives life misnaming has taken away. The Bible shows that this is what is in the heart of God. It's what the prophets say is God's passion: "cease to do evil, learn to do good; seek justice, rescue the oppressed, defend the orphan, plead for the widow" (Is 1:16-17). "See," Jesus said, "I am making all things new" (Rev 21:5). When we truly name one another, we are reflecting the God we worship.

Reflection. *What names do you wish you were given by someone—or what is something you think currently misnames you? What name do you currently use toward someone that you think you need to change in order to name justly and truly? How can you do that? What will help you practice that?*

Sabbath Encouragement

It's time again to pause: more deep breath. No rush. These are demanding subjects. We didn't get where we are overnight, nor will we see the change we want with great ease or speed either. What the gospel of Jesus Christ offers people is the best possible way of naming hope. In a way, the Bible says God could choose to see and name us as we do others, and that would be a "just deserts" sort of outcome. But the astonishing wonder is that that is not what God does. Quite the reverse, and this is the turning point from despair to hope. Peter knew the names he deserved from his Lord, but he also knew the name he was given. Here Peter writes some sabbath encouragement we need to drink in as deeply as we can:

> Come to [Jesus], a living stone, though rejected by mortals yet chosen and precious in God's sight, and like living stones, let yourselves be built into a spiritual house, to be a holy priesthood, to offer spiritual sacrifices acceptable to God through Jesus Christ. For it stands in scripture:
>
> "See, I am laying in Zion a stone,
>> a cornerstone chosen and precious;
> and whoever believes in him will not be put to shame."
>
> To you then who believe, he is precious; but for those who do not believe,
>
> "The stone that the builders rejected
>> has become the very head of the corner,"
>
> and
>
> "A stone that makes them stumble,
>> and a rock that makes them fall."
>
> They stumble because they disobey the word, as they were destined to do.
>
> But you are a chosen race, a royal priesthood, a holy nation, God's own people, in order that you may proclaim the mighty acts of him who called you out of darkness into his marvelous light.

Once you were not a people,
> but now you are God's people;
once you had not received mercy,
> but now you have received mercy. (1 Pet 2:4-10)

1. I encourage you to memorize this text and meditate on it as a reminder of how God delights in giving you a new name with a new hope and a new life. Today and every day we need this salvation and hope again, and that is just what we are provided.

2. I encourage you to take heart that as dark as our misperceiving and misnaming may be, God's capacity to see and name is far greater still. Indeed it is the light that is God's hope to us, and in that light there is no darkness at all (1 Jn 1).

3. I encourage you to embrace the vision and practices of this book as a step into the light which can be shocking or disorienting, but is finally life-giving and sure.

CONFESSION OF SIN

Gracious God, our sins are too heavy to carry, too real to hide, and too deep to undo;

Forgive what we tremble to name, what our bodies can no longer bear;

Forgive us for lives unadjusted to the order of Your love, for hearts out of rhythm with the pulse of Your compassion, for tongues unaccustomed to the shape of confession;

Set us free from a past that we cannot change; open us to a future in which we can be changed, And refashion our expectations to Your Will, that we may grow in grace, and be shaped in Your image.

THE PRESBYTERIAN BOOK OF COMMON WORSHIP (ADAPTED)

Part Four

Acting

Free to Act

God made human beings free—to act. This freedom, one of the mysteries of God's design, leaves open every possibility of doing what can build up life, doing what can destroy it and everything everywhere in between. This surely must be one of the most perplexing parts of a biblical worldview.

If I were God, I am quite sure I wouldn't take this risk, unleash this danger. I would prefer tighter management. Not God. God is willing to create in freedom and to call us to live and love in freedom too. That is God's longing and desire. That is how God, in freedom, chooses to love humanity. Not blind to our folly, not dull to our suffering, not indifferent to our power, God nonetheless gives human beings freedom to act.

We come to the subject of acting at this point not because it is sequentially the last of the three (after perceiving and naming), nor because it is third in importance, but because the visibility of our actions wrongly *inflates* their importance just as the invisibility of our perceiving and naming wrongly *deflates* their importance. Our lives are an inseparable whole; our inner and outer lives are of one piece. Two of Jesus' major themes are the way we try to use actions to mask our inner attitudes (e.g., showing off in our prayers or giving) along with the way our inner attitudes fail to make their way into our actions (e.g., saying "Lord, Lord" but failing to show it). Our God knows us thoroughly and knows that any real commitment to lives of justice in the world requires a comprehensive transformation of the heart: we are those not just who act justly but who reflect in our whole being that we seek and do justice. Likewise that we are not just those with concern for justice but those who act justly and seek justice for the oppressed. God's justice is God's character in action, and so God intends for our character to be just as well.

We are free to act justly, we just don't. In that failure we are unjust toward ourselves even as we are being unjust toward our neighbor. Our inner bankruptcy shows in our public lives by choices and actions everyday.

A few years ago, when the global economy was thriving, private jet travel was on the rise. For those who could afford it in a post-9/11 world, the hassle of commercial air travel was just too much to accept. The alternative was obvious: take a private jet. A feature article explained that a person who always wanted to have this alternative available could preload a credit card with up to $200,000 in order to be ready for those moments when he or she just needed a personal jet.

Eventually the article told the story of one man who had made a gazillion dollars in some enterprise and found the hassles of commercial flying just too much to tolerate. He said the turning point came one day when he was taking a commercial flight from one coast to the other. He was flying first class, and there was, if you can believe it, he said, a woman in business class who had a baby that cried the whole trip. He explained that for him this experience settled it once and for all: he would never fly commercial again. Then he gave us the explanation for his actions: "Because I have realized that the important thing to me is excluding from my life people who might bum me out." That was his mission statement. It explained and ordered his life. It showed up in his actions.

When I first read this, I was—well, I confess—I was self-righteously disgusted. And then, as I considered it further, I was even more disgusted. The problem was that as my disgust quotient rose, I realized I was actually not so unlike this man. Perhaps I don't exercise those attitudes in quite such a brash or elitist way, but I would be lying not to admit that I orchestrate many different parts of my life in order "to exclude from my life [many] who might bum me out." It shows in my actions: where I live, where I play, where I drive, who my friends are, how I travel, how I engage and don't engage. On the surface those things don't seem to be about exclusion. But in honesty, my actions speak louder than my words.

Jesus says our actions always do. Actions are pay dirt. If we want a measure of what is really in our hearts, look at our actions. Whatever we claim about our hearts, their true character is measured by what we do. Or what we fail to do. We may say we love, but it turns out to be a lie if we don't love in action (Mt 7; 25).

This means that everything we considered thus far is writ large in what we see in behavior all around us. It means we can read backward from our actions into our hearts. Even allowing plenty of room for sheer finitude and inadequacy, the daily actions of people all around the world on any given day expose the crisis of their hearts. The crisis, as we have seen, is far from being benign or inconsequential. No, the crisis is that our actions demonstrate the pervasively destructive complicity and power of our hearts in a suffering world.

Human failure to seek a world of justice enables some of *us* to thrive: that is the daily reality of our world. Meanwhile, Jesus said, in essence, "come to me all you who really bum me out, so I can give you true well-being."

EXTERNAL EVIDENCE

Our perceiving and naming defines our acting. These are, of course, not discrete steps; they tumble in and around and upon each other. The intertwining mix of these factors shapes how we act in the world, which also affects how we perceive and name it. And so the cycle goes.

We open the morning paper and read headlines about the rise of human trafficking or congressional debates about torture or reports about the poisoning of baby formula in Asia or land-grabbing from AIDS widows in parts of Africa. Our broad perception is that we consider those issues as not belonging to us. Those issues belong to them. Right there lie the ordinary, false, subtle and profound assumptions that allow injustice to flourish. Our failure to act on these things provides the proof.

In this simple and invisible way, we assume we are not responsible, not key factors, not relevant participants in this problem. We are insignificant and inadequate people surrounded by global need. Geographic, national, racial and economic factors readily filter the steps that might otherwise lead us to act.

Simply put, the problem works this way: if we had the same number of people perpetrating overt and heinous acts of injustice every day, but had a world of more people who were committed to daily acts of justice, sounding a drumbeat of active intolerance for injustice, less suffering would occur.

Is this the same as saying, "If people weren't people, things would be a lot better"? In some ways it is. But the presumption behind that statement is often that our humanity can't or won't change.

Reflection. How do inertia, resignation or paralysis affect your heart's readiness to "do justice" in the world? In what ways are paralysis or resignation a further act of injustice? What can break this cycle in your life or in the lives of others who could make a response but don't?

FACE TO FACE

Today's newspaper, which could have been yesterday's or tomorrow's, displays the predictable evidence we need of an unjust, unloving world. The headlines are noteworthy only in their being the latest expressions of this fundamental experience of daily life around the planet. The shock of it really is that the different stories each day are in so many ways the same stories. From one angle, the stunning thing is the commonality of our human dilemmas more than their variety. "All the news that's fit to print" testifies to what we hold in common: the intrapersonal, interpersonal and international stories of broken glass, etched lenses and shuttered windows.

At one point in writing this, the postelection chaos and violence that overtook western Kenya were getting lots of attention. Here is an excerpt from an email letter I received that morning from the wife of Micah, a young American photojournalist caught in the melee:

> During the night last night, I received a text message from Micah telling me he needed me to register him with the US Embassy in Kenya. During the night, I was on the phone with the US Embassy here and in Kenya. They actually were able to reach him and complete his registration. Receiving this during the night really concerned me as I knew he was planning to be in Nakuru—a place that has recently seen a harsh increase in violence.
>
> This morning he was able to call. It is difficult to summarize all that he said. The situation in Eldoret, where he is now, is really escalating. He was unable to travel to Nakuru because clashes are breaking out within the military which had resulted in a murder the night before they were to leave with the convoy. Micah and Julius (our friend he is with in Eldoret) instead went to a school that had been torched and to the refugee camp which now has twenty thousand people. Devastation is everywhere. Tension is growing.
>
> On their way home, they were caught at a roadblock and found themselves in a really dangerous situation. He said

that their car was surrounded by a huge mob—hundreds of people. Cars were burning just behind them and an even larger mob was running towards them from behind. The mob was all over their car and Micah and Julius had poisoned arrows pointed at them. Micah was hit in the back with a board. He's not sure if it was meant to hit him or the car. Police came and were firing shots and the mob was dispersed. When I spoke to Micah they were at Julius' home. He said houses nearby are on fire, they can hear gunshots, car explosions—chaos.

On the day I received this, I went to a soccer game for our younger son, had burgers at In-N-Out, drove our comfortable, functioning car about twenty miles on various errands, stopped by to see a friend, had fun making dinner as a family, and watched a movie in comfortable chairs in a lovely room on a nice television. Meanwhile, the scene in Kenya was unfolding. What might otherwise have simply been newspaper headlines landed, because of a friendship, in my email box. I know and love people in Kenya, which brings the story that much closer. The violent news on any given day may be exceptional to a particular location, but it is typical of our fractured world. We could change the names and places and find so many contexts in the world today, whether on a large or small scale, for which this same narrative line could be apt.

Given the depth and pervasiveness, the internal and the external distortions in our perceptions and relationships with God, ourselves and one another, what possibilities exist for any of this to change? If injustice lies in every human heart, what hope is there? Is this appeal just a work of fiction?

Scripture realistically conveys the ultimate intractability of our situation if left to our own devices (Rom 3; Jas 1:22-25). God's unfolding revelation offers humanity our only hope: Jesus Christ. The most profound human experience is to love and to be loved. If that is so, it's no wonder our love-starved world is in such crisis. It's no wonder either that God, who made us in and for love, who knows the scarcity and abuse of love, came among us as incarnate love in action to ask us to live and respond to this love.

Following Jesus Christ is not a way out of loving the world but a way into doing so (Jn 17). Well-intentioned persons can will themselves into being more just actors in the world. But without the inner and outer transformation that only God is capable of accomplishing, we are without hope. God alone delivers this from being a work of fiction. It is not a statement about religion, the church or dogma. This names reality.

> **Reflection.** *If the eternal trajectory is "face to face" with God and with one another, our lives here are to reflect and practice this. Make a map of those you see face to face. As you make a series of concentric circles, from those you see directly and clearly to those you barely see at all, what makes the difference in your sight, in your naming and in your actions of living face to face?*

FOR GOD SO LOVED THE WORLD

Faithful worship awakens us to see, name and act in light of reality: God's love for the created order and for all humanity. God's call to Israel has always been centered in this transformative work of worship that reorders our loves to reflect God's. To be faithful to God means living God's love in action. This is the worship God seeks (Is 58).

It seemed to Israel that God was "their God" and by definition not the god of the nations. This played into Israel's assumption that Yahweh was their nationalistic deity, the tribal god whose vested promises and interests were bent toward Israel and away from others.

This narrow, revisionist picture of Yahweh is far less encompassing than even the opening promise of God to Abram, to create a people who will be blessed and by whom the nations are to be blessed as well. It is human nature to be far more interested in the first part of that promise than the second. We are simply more interested in seeing the world and God through our self-interest and tribal interest than through the heart of God (see Amos).

The canon of Scripture makes the case that the particularity of God's love to Israel is for the sake of the universality of God's love for the world. In contrast to the tribal deities and idols of Israel's neighbors, Yahweh is "the God of Abraham, Isaac, and Jacob" and also "Lord of heaven and earth." "Who is like you, O LORD" (Ex 15:11)?

God does not shrink to fit Israel's vision. Israel is called to see the world God's way. But that is more easily said than done. Nowhere is this more evident than over the matter of Israel's desire for a king. They looked at their neighbors who had kings and they wanted one too. Israel seemed to be allured by the notion of a galvanizing, central leader who spoke to and led and guided them (1 Kings).

That vision of a human king became more compelling than the extraordinary reality that God was their King. What Israel had was theocracy, and God (somewhat sheepishly) pointed out to Israel that they had the better deal, unequivocally the better King. But in the end, the smaller, nationalistic, physical leadership of an appointed king captured their hearts. God condescended to provide his people a king, but all the nationalistic myopia and distraction that came with that vision took over. Their fortunes rose and fell based on leadership that was much less reliable than the King who called and promised them blessing. The channel of God's grace was diverted not by the grand vision of the Lord of all but by the vicissitudes of Israel's national life (see 1-2 Kings).

Babylon as "the other" forced itself in shocking and redefining ways on Israel. The issue within this new context was whether Israel would demonstrate that it belonged to Yahweh or to these foreigners. Would Israel come to see the world as Babylon sees itself and the world, or would this exilic life clarify the distinctive vision that was Yahweh's for who they were and how Babylon should be seen?

As represented in the book of Daniel, in the face of Nebuchadnezzar's anxiety over his dream of being deposed, God provided Daniel with insight into the dream and its interpretation. What Daniel affirmed in his prayer was that Yahweh alone is the One who could raise up kings and depose them. What Daniel declared to Nebuchadnezzar was that no human had the ability both to tell of the dream and to give its interpretation. But the God who Daniel worshiped could provide trustworthy spiritual insight. Then God through Daniel boldly went on to tell Nebuchadnezzar the dire news of the demise of the king's kingdom. Daniel was seeing beyond the boundaries of power as defined by Babylon and its tyrant.

The book of Hosea is another anguished love song for Israel during this same exilic time. Israel had been the harlot, and still God's love was not stopped. Here we see as bold and suffering an image of God's love as we find anywhere in the Old Testament. So it was not the Babylonian foreigners who were the prostitute but Israel itself, the blessed people of God. And still God loved them.

This forms the backdrop to what eventually emerges as the stunning evidence from the Gospels that "God so loved the world that he gave his only Son, so that everyone who believes in him may not perish but may have eternal life" (Jn 3:16). Jesus is the fulfillment of the identity of Israel, the one who is blessed and through whom, from then on, the blessing is passed to the nations, to Jerusalem, to Judea and Samaria and to the ends of the earth (Acts 1:8). In Paul's words, "to the Jew first, and also to the Greek" (Rom 1:16).

From the opening genealogy of Matthew to the closing chapter of Revelation, we are offered a vision of God's love that seeks a lost and broken world, including but not limited to Israel. It's the narrative of the fulfillment of God's promise to them for the salvation of Israel and of the world. Jesus himself displays and enacts God's overflowing, unrestricted love that pours out toward those not otherwise included. The mandate of Luke 4 affirms the vision of Isaiah 61 and points toward a ministry that breaks boundaries and flows out to the social margins.

Jesus offended people by what he said, as well as by what he did. He touched, ate, healed, named, loved, celebrated, listened, served and died for all the wrong people. The woman at the well knew it. So did Nicodemus (Jn 3). So did Joseph of Arimathea (Mt 27:57). So did the woman who touched the hem of his garment (Lk 8:42-47). So did Matthew (Mt 9). So did the man born blind and his parents (Jn 9). So did the Gerasene demoniac (Lk 8:26-39). Jesus acted. And that was a problem.

This is the shock of Jesus' call to his disciples. He was always seeing people differently from how his disciples did. He stopped to see those who could have been ignored. He remembered, in age, lifestyle, circumstances, spiritual condition, those on whom many around him closed the shutters. Jesus relentlessly opens the shutters and says, "Look again . . . with my heart and mind." This act of paying attention is the core of our discipleship, proof of our worship and evidence that our shuttered windows are now open and opening wider still.

The places and people from whom we might turn away are those to whom, in Christ, we are meant to turn. In the places of injustice, suffering, need and death, we are meant to look and see, love and serve. This is the new vision that comes from worshiping the One who wants our vision to reflect his.

This extends itself in Pentecost and in the multilingual voice of the good news. This is the disorientation of Peter's dream and the graphic redepiction of who is included in the blessing of God (Acts 10). This is the prelude to Paul's mission to the Gentiles. Seeing the world no longer through the mark of circumcision but through the embrace of God's love in Christ that calls people of every tribe, tongue and nation into a new humanity, into a world of God's justice and mercy.

Reflection. If this is God's way of seeing, naming and acting, what implications are there for us in addition to our own personal salvation? If we are God's plan for showing this reality, what does it compel you to consider and to do differently in the world? Especially, what will you do toward those least prone to see or know the evidence of such love and justice? Who can encourage you in this? Who can you encourage? How?

HELEN AND MICHAEL

Helen was on her way into a store. An exceptionally unclean man panhandled her as she was trying to enter, and this time Helen felt moved and ready to respond. Actually, Helen smelled this man before she saw him. With her senses a bit overwhelmed, she took out a $5 bill and carefully extended it to its full length so as to avoid touching the man, attempting to hand it to him. As she did so, the man not only came closer but enveloped her in a bear hug that lasted one minute but seemed like ten.

Discombobulated, Helen shuffled a bit and, after brief mutual introductions, went on her way. Michael was his name, and profusely grateful would not be too strong a description of his response to her gift.

Later, it occurred to Helen that she couldn't remember Michael's face; she had to admit to herself that she had deliberately avoided really looking at him, especially looking him full on in the eyes. Out of her sense of what it meant to follow Jesus, she felt she really needed to look at Michael, not to wimp out but to extend to him her typically genuine and open-faced way of greeting people in her daily life.

The next time she went to the store, she looked for Michael in order to take the time and express the dignity he deserved by actually looking him in the eyes. This happened. They had a warm greeting and Helen continued on with her shopping.

Now some months beyond these early encounters, Helen can say that she has actually come to love and care for Michael, and to see him very differently from how she had at the start. He is a real person, with real relationships and circumstances, facing real needs and able to both receive and offer real compassion to Helen and to others.

Michael is no longer simply the unseen but smelly man near the entrance to the store. Michael, in relation to Helen, is someone far more than she dared initially encounter, and she is far more than he usually sees either. Both are changed. Both are more truly themselves by how they see and how they are seen. They are living more of the love of God by loving one another.

> **Reflection.** *What do you learn from the story of Helen and Michael? What has it transformed? Why? What action could you take to show a similar love? Who do you not want to engage and truly see and name? If you think you should do otherwise, what are some first steps you could take?*

GOD'S CONTAGION OF HOPE

It takes only the first eleven chapters of Genesis to raise the implicit, if confounding and fearful, question: Is there hope for a world like ours? In Genesis 12 God does not respond with a display of awesome power. Instead, God makes a promise.

To Abram, God says,

> Go from your country and your kindred and your father's house to the land that I will show you. I will make of you a great nation, and I will bless you, and make your name great,

so that you will be a blessing. I will bless those who bless you, and the one who curses you I will curse; and in you all the families of the earth shall be blessed. (Gen 12:1-3)

Humanity is not abandoned in the crisis. But neither are we offered what we might wish for or would have designed were we in charge: an all-encompassing, plainly evident "fix." Perhaps we might have imagined some fundamental retooling of human freedom, acknowledging that what seemed a good idea initially was too extreme, too risky, too much weight on too small a frame. Or maybe we would have wished for a more dramatic reconception of the human heart, seeing our evident arrhythmias making our lives too unstable, too prone to quiet acts of desperation.

God chooses a promise. This is among the earliest evidences in Scripture that God's thoughts are not our thoughts and God's ways are not our ways. Counterintuitive does not begin to capture what seems on God's part to be an approach that seems absurd, underwhelming and irrelevant. Herein begins the scandal that will one day become its most exquisite expression: the cross.

God's response to the human condition is to make a promise that is personal, particular, relational, gift-giving, boundary-setting and inclusive. For those who would have wished for surgery, remodeling or an army, this is not what God offers. Instead, God does what God does: God treats Israel like the people he wants them to become. And that sets the stage for a very, very long story.

Clearly God sees something we do not. He names something we would never name in the same way. Yet Abram becomes Abraham by trusting the difference and leaning into God's way rather than his own. God chooses and makes promises to Abram, but what he sees is not only about Abram but about Abram as a person who begins the story of a new people with an end that will bring God's well-being to God's people, and eventually to people everywhere.

This is God's way of taking the problem of evil seriously and personally. To us, this is a tediously slow, largely invisible work of transformation. This is a one-heart-at-a-time, one-people-at-a-time approach. If this is a new mirror, in place of the broken ones we use to perceive ourselves and one another, God's method is certainly not ours.

God does not, for example, look at the human situation and see it with the same urgency we do. We feel justified in crying "Fire! Fire!" but God apparently does not. Our sense of timeliness, whether on an individual or global scale, is baffled, at times angered, by this approach on God's part. The meaning of the parts and of the whole both matter and are entirely in God's view, Scripture indicates, but it does not lead him to the fretful, anxious urgency it does us.

God's approach moves from the particular to the universal and is the opposite of what many of us might have purposed. Our instincts are to want God to take large, dramatic steps to eliminate the possibility of evil and suffering, for example. That would seem sensible, obvious, compelling. For reasons hinted at but never fully described, however, God does not respond this way.

God's encompassing plan to make all things right starts with a promise to a person and a people, an enacted demonstration in word and then in deed, of the character and purposes God has for humanity. What is radical is not a change of physical, emotional, social circumstances per se, although Abram's call to leave his home is part of the transformation God seeks. In the end Ur is new to Abram, but it is not an intrinsically more faithful domain.

The most significant alteration God initiates is the call on Abram for his life to be lived in the domain of God's promise. From God's point of view, this is the most urgent change, the starting point for everything else. It's there that human freedom and human relationship as God intends them to be can thrive. We might call it theological environmentalism. It's conservation and restoration for the sake of transformation. It's about being with God and God being with Abram and his descendents. From God's point of view this changes life's fundamental terms. In God's economy, this particularity contains hope for the whole.

> **Reflection.** *Hope is typically caught and stimulated like a healthy contagion. Does anyone exemplify living this way to you? Are you prepared to seek to live this way—to move forward to preempt negative naming and take new actions that reflect the justice and love of God?*

ON THE WAY

No man ever saw God and lived. And yet, I shall not live till I see God; and when I have seen Him, I shall never die. (John Donne)

To glorify God means to reflect the reality of God, to demonstrate the reality of God in all we do. This means we begin to perceive through the lens of God's love, truth and justice, in place of the shattered glass we know so well. It is to engage in a long process of changing vision. It's a matter of the heart, of transformation from the inside out—difficult, slow, personal change. It's mending work. It involves reclamation as well as replacement. It requires patience and demands practice.

The more I look at the love of Jesus, the more my own capacity to love grows. The more I am with others who love in ways God loves, the more I desire to love that way too. That's why we need one another so much. My jaded heart can be softened when I dare to let someone who really loves show me how they see what I may not. People I know who are nurses, doctors, lawyers, social workers, teachers, counselors, human-rights advocates, city officials, pastors, missionaries and more are among those who teach me to see differently. They carry perspectives of people in need that can help change the way I look at the people around me. It increases my willingness to look, to be curious, to presuppose that things are not necessarily as they appear, that it would be good to remember that I don't see nearly as well as I think I do.

So too do my relationships with people who by any measure are poor and oppressed. It's time with people at a shelter, in a food project, in a tutoring program, in a rehab facility, in an aftercare facility, in a slum, in an HIV support group, in a prison or in the shelter they call home that allows daily experiences of injustice to become much clearer. Our hearts and actions have a chance to change in significant ways.

I have been helped to see more clearly by listening to the way others describe what they see. For example, *28: Stories of AIDS in Africa* by Stephanie Nolen is a stunning example. You can't write as she does without first seeing as she does. Her twenty-eight stories can be read like guided tours into careful, nuanced, loving, gentle, honoring, compassionate vision. Her book deals with the lives of people with AIDS, which is her primary purpose. I find that deliberately reading writers who see well is very fruitful in my own capacity to see.

Our only hope for clearer and deeper vision is grace. But we receive such grace usually by acting, asking for it and taking steps to receive it. Admitting our need for a renewed mirror per se does not produce hope. Nor does sorrow over our inescapably distorted vision. Grace does and must come along the way.

All of us once lived among them in the passions of the flesh, following the desires of flesh and senses, and we were by nature children of wrath, like everyone else. But God, who is rich in mercy, out of the great love with which he loved us even when we were dead through our trespasses, made us alive together with Christ—by grace you have been saved—and raised us up with him and seated us with him in the heavenly places in Christ Jesus, so that in the ages to come he might show the immeasurable riches of his grace in kindness toward us in Christ Jesus. For by grace you have been saved through faith, and this is not your own doing; it is the gift of God—not the result of works, so that no one may boast. For we are what he has made us, created in Christ Jesus for good works, which God prepared beforehand to be our way of life. (Eph 2:3-10)

In apostle Paul's graphic depiction, he calls our circumstances nothing less than being dead in our trespasses (Eph 2:1). He names the shattered, hopeless mirrors that we and others are. This reality is what makes the converse of it all, God's gift of grace and life, beyond our wildest hopes and imaginations. We are saved by God's grace. By the One who sees most clearly and most powerfully, we are delivered from our deadness and brought into a new context: "raised . . . up with [Christ] and seated . . . with him in the heavenly places in Christ" (Eph 2:6). This is no act of human skill or ingenuity, "so that no one may boast" (Eph 2:9). Taking credit would be the opposite of clear vision, an expression of continued blindness—not sight.

This would be the situation of the unforgiving servant Jesus speaks about (Mt 18:23-35). In this parable the man who owes a staggering obligation is forgiven his entire debt. But despite the personal benefit of this grace, the man is incapable of extending it to someone who owes him a small debt. Grace, it turns out, does not work automatically or unilaterally. Grace must be the start of what then must be allowed to make its way into every corner of our lives.

What Jesus wanted for the forgiven servant was not just to be forgiven but, out of his forgiveness, to see and live forgivingly. This is God's endless hope for those whom he loves and forgives. He treats us in the way he wants us to treat ourselves and one another. From the promise to Abraham onward, that's straightforward.

My life has changed and continues to change because of friends and others I know who are so much further down the road of acting these things out than I am. Whether or not we share similar cultural starting points or life experiences, people I know call me into a new and different life.

One of the most profound examples of these people in my life is a woman named Judy. She had one of the most hellacious childhoods of anyone I have personally known. The physical, emotional and sexual abuse she suffered was more than enough to close off any basic human normalcy in her. Then she met the God of intimate and healing grace. Still, she could have understandably and easily chosen to live the rest of her life as a victim, now comforted by Jesus, but shattered and comatose. Instead, she gradually embraced and leads a ministry to young girls and women who have been through their own hell. She serves with freedom and passion. For Judy, it turns out that her early story is not the most important story of her life, nor her suffering the worst to be experienced. She acts this out every day, not just in relation to those she expressly serves but also as a person who lives in ordinary time and interacts with ordinary people. She is someone whose heart of bitterness has become a fresh, flowing stream of kindness. This is the fruit of her life of worship.

AN OFFERING OF ABUNDANCE AND INADEQUACY

When we set aside time to worship privately or corporately, what we need then is deep and regular meditation on the character, love, mercy and justice of God. The reason for becoming familiar with the whole Bible, as well as for spending time focused on Jesus' ministry in the four Gospels, is to let ourselves be shaped by these images and narratives. Then we can pray for and support one another in taking small steps on any given day or week to let those vignettes shape our responses to the people we encounter.

Out of such reflection can flow worship, which needs to be a personal, ordinary, daily act. It's also meant to be part of what the people of God regularly do together. Each reciprocally affects the other. Some of the important grist of worship for me has been developing acts through every day of offering myself to God for whatever purposes and activities the day may hold. I try to practice praying actively throughout the day, constantly offering up silent prayers of dependency and responsiveness to God's purposes. It's like a running subtext:

"Lord, open and soften my heart today. You have been so generous toward me. May I give out of all I have and even out of what I think I don't have. Help me to see and respond to my neighbor as you do. Use and meet me as I walk down the street, stand in line, engage with friends who live on the street, in the classroom where I tutor, as I wait at the Social Security office for an elderly friend who is difficult to be with or as I write to my city council representative about the crack house I know about. Use my gifts and life as I am working, playing, relaxing. Take my time. Take my money. Take my power. Take my powerlessness. Take my weariness. Take my fears. Take my tongue. Take my questions. All that I have and all that I don't have are in your hands."

Reflection. If we don't know what we see until we act on our vision, what steps are you taking to test and develop, to refine and improve your vision by acting? What bold new act for the next season of life are you sensing that God may be asking you to make for the sake of justice and mercy toward those suffering and in need?

Suffering

What we are offered, and indeed given, is grace upon grace, the difference between death and life. But we can and do stop its infusion.

GRACE UPON GRACE

Over the long covenant that is Yahweh's relationship to Israel, and Israel's relationship with Yahweh, the grace that is given does not work its way into the heart pervasively enough. Like the unforgiving servant, this inconsistency seems almost unimaginable when seen from the outside. It begs for Israel to make a different response. It makes us cry, "Why don't *they* get it?"

Until, as Jesus intended, we realize that the question is actually, "Why don't *we* (the church) get it?" Christian history is not just littered but filled with Jesus' followers failing to pass on what they have been given. We could point to the large, public displays of this disjunction, such as the defense of slavery, the abuse of women, the Inquisitions, the Crusades, or the church's silence and even participation in various genocides. All that would be indicting enough.

More frequently, however, we could just point to ordinary, daily acts of prejudice, hatred, disdain, neglect, indifference and self-absorption revealing that, if we have received grace, we have hoarded it (Ex 16). We cannot hoard without something in or around us rotting. We proclaim a gospel that transforms us from life to death, from crushing debt to joyful liberation, but it does not actually seem to change our vision or our hearts. If it does not do that, what good is it?

In my own life, I wonder how this can be so. From the time I was a college student and had some of my earliest exposure to the teaching of Jesus and his compelling truthfulness, I was aware of my need. I felt known by Jesus as he would interact with those around him in the Gospels. The issues he named in their lives felt as if they were mine too—I may not have liked it, and often bristled as I first read them, but I still felt seen and named.

I eventually came to the point of laying down my resistance. Then I could hear the good news that Jesus saw and named me in love for the sake of my salvation. He delivered me from my petty and broken self—but it was not for my sake alone. God's grace was for the sake of loving others as well, especially as one who was discovering what it was to long to be fully known, fully loved, and who was finding that in the embrace of Jesus Christ.

Still, something akin to an unforgiving servant's heart—a heart that doesn't really get it—has too often been my story. Not in especially heinous or grievous forms for the most part. Just letting my cultural and educational background, my gender and race, my class and position give me all the reasons I need to be parsimonious about justice.

This is the way it is with the majority of us who live as part of a dominant culture. In general we find our lives acceptable, not getting all we might desire but having most of what we need. Our rage against the machine is occasional, but seldom about matters that are dire for others who are helpless. Most days, justice issues are not on our agenda. Justice has been built into systems that benefit us, that put us in places where we get what we expect or deserve or need, and often more. We don't wish others to be deprived of these things, but we grow complacent in our awareness that the justice we count as normative simply does not exist for others; we wish them no evil, but we do them no good. In the end it amounts to a life that assumes the blessing for ourselves without either the urgency or the passion to seek it for others.

> **Reflection.** How clearly do you think you see your own privilege? What are examples of that in your daily life? Is it racial? Cultural? Educational? Economic? These can be gifts that help us see more accurately sometimes, but they can as readily be blinders. What disciplines and actions could you take over the next few weeks to practice seeing, naming and acting less out of privilege and more out of gratitude for grace and justice?

TURNING POINT

A couple of years ago at the First Presbyterian Church of Berkeley's Global Church Conference, we heard from Bishop David Zac Niringiye from Kampala, Uganda. Earlier that evening we had shown *The Invisible Children*, a film about the horror of the suffering of children abducted as soldiers in northern Uganda and of the night-commuter camps where thousands of children went to sleep together each evening in order to avoid the same kind of abduction and torture. This gripping story led people that night to ask understandably: "What should we do for those children in northern Uganda?" Bishop Zac replied, "You won't know what to do until they are first your children."

He was saying that the first step should not be to brainstorm possible solutions to help the children in northern Uganda. What we need instead is first to reframe who these children are in relation to us. Then our responses might actually land in the places they may be most needed, with the passions and commitment that might make a difference.

In other words, the problem needs to move from the abstract to the personal, from the aggregate to the individual, from concern for "abducted or night-commuting children" to "my abducted or night-commuting children." We may then feel even more overwhelmed, inadequate and uncertain. But we would no longer be distant. What's more is we could no longer even imagine being paralyzed. The reality we would then have stepped into wouldn't allow us to indulge that. Injustice would not just have moved more deeply into our awareness; injustice would have moved into our lives. And that makes the difference.

Indeed, it makes too much difference. We want to care about injustice, but we don't want to embrace it as a reality that comes all the way into our lives. Most of us at the conference that night would have preferred that Bishop Zac let us off with a to-do list of ways we could change lives of children in northern Uganda. What he did instead was call us to a level of engagement that would change our lives as well. That's more than we were asking for.

What this exposes is not easy to face or neutral in its implications. We are located in racial, economic, class and political settings that almost always serve our interests. The hard wiring of our cultural and social location has partitioned us off from the daily suffering of injustice, and we would frankly prefer the deficiency of tokenism to the actuality of pain.

Besides, on what grounds could we say that the children in northern Uganda are "our children"? Bishop Zac was certainly not advocating a new paternalism or colonization, but awareness of our common, shared, interdependent humanity. All the more, if we see and name our neighbor as Jesus does.

Many of us were then motivated, as an act of worship, to become more educated about the situation in northern Uganda, to think and pray and act on behalf of those children every day. Like yellow ribbons to remind us of others facing desperate circumstances, we posted pictures of those suffering in northern Uganda in our sanctuary so that as we met for corporate worship we realized our doing so was about more than merely ourselves. We prayed for them as we gathered on Sundays and through the week. Some of us subscribed to online newspapers from Uganda. Some of us made our screensaver pictures of people in northern Uganda so we looked at their faces every day. As a personal habit I began as a part of my personal devotions each morning to write a brief letter of appeal and concern to various political or governmental offices regarding northern Uganda. These were all simple expressions of worship that helped deliver us from the fiction of our self-focused world and took us closer to seeing, naming and acting in light of reality.

> **Reflection.** *Our hearts are changed when we are prepared to identify with those in need—enter, share, step inside. Are you doing this? What could be your next step? Where do you notice you get most easily stopped? Why? What do you think that tells you about the challenge of your own transformation? Are there people you know who are inspiring to you in this area of your own need?*

TWO LETTERS

It's one thing to acknowledge injustice, and quite another to be gripped by it. What is still more unusual is to take steps to change it. The difference usually has to do with several factors: the degree of urgency, combined with our sense of the problem's personal relevance, and our confidence about having an impact. How we "see and name" paralyzes or promotes the chances that we will respond.

The more personally disconnected, distant or fearsome the injustice may be, the more difficult it is to feel any capacity to respond. This fact alone shapes so much of human experience, whether the boy crying wolf is in our home or next door or on the other side of the world. Even when it is a real wolf and at the door daily, we manage that news by dulling our perception, as long as it is *their* problem.

World hunger is a defining daily experience for millions. I can know this, understand it, be worried about it and still hold it at great distance. The phrase *starving child* becomes different with the addition of the simple word *my*. The truth of hunger has not been changed by the addition of that small pronoun—but by the addition of one word, the injustice of world hunger lands forcefully in our lives. The actual injustice is the same, but the confidence that something *must be done* is immediate and unequivocal.

Real wolves are at the doors of countless people everyday. They could each say in the face of some injustice, this is "my" story and therefore it has the relevance and urgency to warrant a response. In fact, many people would say this is *our* story, because they don't think so individualistically and because most forms of injustice are collective more than individual.

The difference between "starving child" and "my starving child" is as different as "their starving child" is from "our starving child." If all starving children are God's, then in some sense all starving children are also ours. Our invisible acts of perception and naming are so influential in creating the difference that hangs on *them* and *us*. Those categories are insidious in shaping the character and distribution of injustice. They are frequently pronouncements as powerful as life or death itself.

"Their genocide . . . their bonded slavery . . . their wrongful imprisonment . . . their AIDS" pushes away from me and us the poignancy of their injustice. I don't see them as compassionately, as humanly, as empathetically as I see those closest to me. Of course not, we might plead. Of course we can't and don't see the suffering of others in the same way we see and name our own. That's the point: it's not ours.

We could call this perspective the order of the day, one that stretches as far back in history as we might go, and as far into the future as we might project. It can seem benign when it is an expression of our finitude. We might, at times, wish we were omnipresent, but we are not. "The survival of the fittest" grooms us to look after our own survival first. Part of living humanly is acknowledging our limits, not pretending or projecting that we can do more than we can.

The difficulty tragically fused with our finitude is our all-encompassing self-interest. It's not easily possible even to imagine the former without the latter. Meanwhile, injustice is chronic.

> **Reflection.** *Focus on some headline crisis of need in the world and personalize your relationship to the concern (e.g., "my brother in Darfur," "my cousin with AIDS in Malawi," "my friend uncharged but imprisoned in Manila"). Write your thoughts and feelings and actions and how they are changed by "my."*

THE TEACHER

We are going along in our life, and then, suddenly, enter stage left, right or center: suffering. Loss, pain, inadequacy or failure strike us. However and why these experiences come our way, they sometimes leave us changed, more awake, more alert, more sensitive. They can also leave us disabled, temporarily or longer; they can cause us to withdraw or to hide.

Suffering is no virtue in biblical faith, but it seems to be an inherent part of coming to share in the heart of Jesus. The heart of God toward the world is a compassionate but suffering heart. It's not principally the ebullience of rosy-cheeked compassion, but more the tear-stained heart of our suffering God who enters into our need.

We usually discuss suffering as the problem itself. Here I want to express cautiously, tenderly and carefully that suffering has a part in helping us gain new hearts. This is not treating it with a sleight of hand; it is not glossing the problem of pain. Rather, I want to suggest that some of what enables us to grow requires having our hearts break.

This is no romanticized angst. But we will often be better able to enter the pain of others if we have suffered ourselves. Life usually provides us with this opportunity unsolicited. As an act of following Jesus we can also embody compassion as a spiritual fruit both of Jesus' pain on our behalf and possibly of our own pain as well. It usually takes suffering to teach us that we can make a decision to love that includes suffering because we know that the love of God for us was not stopped in our pain, nor should we let it stop our compassion toward others.

One place where the apostle Paul is the most candid and self-disclosing comes at the start of 2 Corinthians. By this point in his ministry Paul has faced staggering difficulties. He now writes to the church at Corinth and shares his heart:

> Blessed be the God and Father of our Lord Jesus Christ, the Father of mercies and the God of all consolation, who consoles us in all our affliction, so that we may be able to console those who are in any affliction with the consolation with which we ourselves are consoled by God. For just as the sufferings of Christ are abundant for us, so also our consolation is abundant through Christ. If we are being afflicted, it is for your consolation and salvation; if we are being consoled, it is for your consolation, which you experience when you patiently endure the same sufferings that we are also suffering. Our hope for you is unshaken; for we know that as you share in our sufferings, so also you share in our consolation.
>
> We do not want you to be unaware, brothers and sisters, of the affliction we experienced in Asia; for we were so utterly, unbearably crushed that we despaired of life itself. Indeed, we felt that we had received the sentence of death so that we would rely not on ourselves but on God who raises the dead.

He who rescued us from so deadly a peril will continue to
rescue us; on him we have set our hope that he will rescue us
again, as you also join in helping us by your prayers, so that
many will give thanks on our behalf for the blessing granted
us through the prayers of many. (2 Cor 1:3-11)

This text is not about some kind of heroic suffering or about pain
as a goal of spiritual valor. Paul writes honestly about the fact that
to live following Christ means, as Jesus himself affirmed, that to
take up our cross and follow him will include suffering.

To learn to be attentive to God in times of suffering involves
learning to see more than just ourselves or the overwhelming fore-
ground of our lives. We must lean into the suffering enough to dare
to discern God's presence and activity in the midst of confusion.
This can itself demand a dramatic act of faith and trust, not least
in the face of all the counterevidence. Just as the resurrection
teaches us that death does not have the final word, so we can learn
in the midst of pain that it does not hold the final word either.

I can write these words only because I have had to learn them by
experience. Much of the time I have learned their truthfulness
through the witness of family and friends who have opened their
lives to me and allowed me to see something of their suffering and
anguish. That is surely one of the greatest honors of being a friend
or a brother in Christ, let alone a pastor.

Within those experiences of others' suffering, however, I have
my own. This is true in small and ordinary ways: failings, tempta-
tions, confusion, injuries, disappointments, sadness. It has also
been true in more extended and dramatic times I can only call
"dark nights of the soul." To feel wholly consumed by defeat, sorrow, regret, loneliness, fear, self-accusation, despair and darkness
is no stranger to me. I have stood at that cliff on many occasions,
and a few times I have fallen into the valley.

One of these times occurred when I was in seminary. Too many classes, a swing-shift job in a discouraging place, no money, no car, no sense of flexibility or hope, no satisfying direction for my studies, a near-deathbed experience for my father, a sense of dissonance between my inner and outer life all led me into despair. I was anxious, fearful, suicidal.

It changed for me in the actions of two friends and their invitation to Thanksgiving lunch. I had no intention of going because I felt so terrible. I had no way of going because I had no car. Thanksgiving was a faraway place. I was not sure I would be alive. But it was these two friends who asked me to lunch. They urged me. They picked me up and drove me. They welcomed me. I vividly remember my reserve about the whole venture as I got into their car. But I remember more vividly still walking into their house through the back door (in part to avoid the social awkwardness of entry through the front door), and into the pantry. I was stopped, transfixed by what I saw on the counters—the makings of the day's feast: pies, rolls, sweet potatoes, white potatoes, green vegetables, jams, olives, butter and the aroma of a roasting turkey with stuffing. For a few moments, I was alone in this chamber of care.

What would have seemed ordinary on most Thanksgiving Days appeared to me on this occasion to be the bread of life. It was an embodied, tangible act of personal love that included even me. I was gradually drawn through the warm, aromatic creativity happening in the kitchen, and into the dining room where I stood overwhelmed as I took in their beautifully set table, wedding gifts from earlier that year now arrayed in warm hospitality. My friends had been imagining this day, preparing for their guests, washing and chopping, planning and anticipating, buying and tasting, concocting and savoring. Writing this even now, so many years later, still brings me to tears. It was the table of hope. And it helped change my darkness.

Intangibly and tangibly, then and in other times since, I have eventually been caught by the grace of God. If that had not been so, I doubt I would be here to write these words. I do not take God's gift of love for granted. Nor could I imagine it was given for my sake alone. I have no nostalgia for such anguish. I want to learn from pain what I can, but I do not want to nurse it. I have learned something of the need to sit with such seasons as long as seems appropriate and necessary, even as I skeptically yearn for times to breathe deeply again, to practice God's invitation to walk in the "broad place" (Ps 18:19) of God's grace. It helps when others make that invitation real by how they act. My two friends taught me that lives can be saved on a Thursday at lunch. I have tried to act that out ever since.

It would not be possible for me to know truly how such experiences have shaped me, but to adapt Helen Keller's phrase, I know that I can now come nearer to tasting the salt of others' tears. My heart is certainly larger and more responsive than it was before. To be aware of my profound neediness means that I have something less to offer than I might otherwise think. In the end it means by God's grace having something better to bring with me as I come alongside others in need as well.

Reflection. Whose suffering are you sharing at this point in your reflections? How did that come to be so? What forms does your love take? How have you been sharing in the suffering or pain of others? How much further do you think you need to be willing to go in doing so?

Practicing Dignity

Both pain and grace are used by God to change our hearts, to extend our capacity to love, even when the price of such love may be high. In some mysterious way the triune communion of God—Father, Son and Spirit—shares our lives and enters into our suffering and need.

THE CALL TO PRACTICE

A friend of Mother Teresa said that people have often presumed that Mother Teresa's call to the poorest of the poor came from her seeing the needs of the poor in Calcutta and her heart simply going out in sacrifice. He said it wasn't like that. It was instead that she entered the heart of Jesus, and therefore she couldn't but help come to the poor and vulnerable. This priest's point is a significant, if not a universal, one, not just as a fact of Mother Teresa's biography, but as an expression of the primary current of love and justice that is God's heart. Our compassion, mercy and justice are true and life-seeking insofar as they are a reflection of the heart of God.

Left to our own devices, human beings feebly and anemically reflect the heart of God. Unless God's heart heals, transforms and empowers us, our default setting will be to respond to injustice in terms that reflect the personal and sociological facts of our lives, possibly with little or no sense of sharing the passion of God to seek justice.

The call to follow Jesus is in part the call to practice living in the heart of God. This was the point of Jesus' call to the Twelve. "Follow me" was Jesus' invitation into a new life to imitate, see, name and act in ways that mirror the heart and mind of God. As the disciples followed, they practiced this new life. It was not natural to them, any more than it is to us.

That life was full of the unexpected and often the undesired. Following Jesus meant stopping to see and care for the woman with the flow of blood when every religious and social expectation was to rush on to the house of Jairus, rather than to see, name and heal the unseen woman. It meant seeing Jesus call out to and then accept the table hospitality of Zacchaeus, the undesirable tax man. It meant becoming flushed with anxiety when Jesus excoriated scribes and Pharisees as he redefined what matters in the reign of God.

The disciples' hearts went where our hearts also go: away from Jesus' instincts of love and justice. They were scandalized, argumentative, embarrassed, clueless, offended, adamant, dismissive, distracted. Just as we are. Their hearts moved toward the hope of power, not toward self-emptying. Their hearts moved toward those who had stature and away from those who did not. Their hearts named crudely and ungraciously rather than truly and graciously. God's thoughts are not our thoughts, and God's ways are not our ways (Is 55:8). God's heart is not our heart.

This underlines the urgency of worship. God *deserves* worship—because of every dimension of God's character, revelation and re-creation. We *need* worship—because it is the central catalyst in remaking our hearts to mirror God's.

Corporate and individual worship practices matter for many reasons, but for no more important reason than this. As the apostle Paul put it, "I appeal to you therefore, brothers and sisters, by the mercies of God, to present your bodies as a living sacrifice, holy and acceptable to God, which is your spiritual worship" (Rom 12:1). Placing ourselves regularly in contexts where we deliberately seek God's transforming, renewing grace is a vital spiritual exercise. This means the Holy Spirit is transforming our hearts and minds, replacing the mirror by which we see ourselves, one another and God.

Jesus also modeled with the disciples that our transformation involves stepping into actual lives and relationships with people in need. He used parables and metaphors to illustrate ways he wants us to live. The Bible is a tool God uses to teach us to live godly lives (2 Tim 3:16). If our hearts' mirrors are going to be renewed, it will mean practicing lives that do justice, love kindness and walk humbly with our God (Mic 6:8). Those are not words about attitude but action. In one way or another, this call demands we get out of our chairs and act.

> **Reflection.** *Are you out of your chair? Where are you practicing doing justice? What are your practices showing you? How and why?*

WHAT GOD SEES, GOD GIVES

God sees us and says we are "very good," that we are "fearfully and wonderfully made." The imprimatur of the *imago Dei* lies at the core of each of our lives and shines from the heart of God into every human life. It's the homing marker that makes us unmistakably God's and unmistakably ourselves.

The *imago Dei* is what the taxonomy of God's heart is calibrated to see and to love. It calibrates the vision God has of each human being in relation to creation, to themselves, to their neighbor and to God as well. In human relations from Dalit to Brahmin, from hoi polloi to elite, from plain to sophisticated, from slave to union worker, we are attuned to a distorted taxonomy, to a diminished vision of what and who really matter.

Meanwhile God desires to renew what we see only on the surface: "They look on the outward appearance, but the LORD looks on the heart" (1 Sam 16:7). What God sees is the treasure of each individual, the dignity and potential planted in each life, the vulnerability and poignancy. God made us for intimacy with others, for flourishing, just relationships in a re-created world.

This does not mean God is blind to pragmatic realities and the lenses of our own vision; he sees our distorted vision perfectly.

God looks on the inside and outside, the obvious and the subtle. The gentle gesture, the unspoken dream, the joy of each of our lives; God witnesses all this with celebration and pride. The flash of intellectual discovery or of artistic creativity, the curiosity that cares for someone or something around us, the dignity through which we display the beauty of our Creator; all this God sees with love. The compassion and sacrifice within family, between friends, amid strangers, toward enemies—all are further evidence of God's vision.

God never misses what is ambiguous, shadowed, dark or invisible. There is no place and no thing, no person and no detail that God does not witness with love and justice. Every sorrow, loneliness, uncertainty, fear, ambivalence or anxiety is pixilated in God's tender heart. Every moment of abuse, violence, war and hatred touches God's heart as well. No terror or darkness is so great that it keeps God from seeing and caring. Every person is on God's list of those he knows, desires and loves.

How do we know all this? Because of God's revelation in creation, in the covenant with Abraham and his descendents, in the law and the prophets, and supremely in Jesus Christ, witnessed to in Scripture—now made known to our hearts by the Holy Spirit.

How will the wider world know? By how the people of God, filled with the Spirit, see and name the world in God's compassionate ways, serving the One who will forever see us through Jesus Christ. This is the good news of our hope and redemption.

We, God's people, are to see, name and love in God's way. That we do not do so is hardly news. That we can become those who live like this is our calling, the hope to which we must turn.

Reflection. *Find a photograph of someone in need that especially captures your attention. Using this picture as a kind of icon of vulnerability, spend five to ten minutes each day this week meditating on the photograph. Try to imagine, feel, share in what you can infer about that person's life. What are the most difficult aspects of his or her experience for you to imagine? What is easier? Why? How would you feel if you were that individual?*

The Act of Worship

The social realities of injustice are an outward and visible sign of an inward and invisible lie. The soulish soil of injustice develops as we are unknowingly shaped by legacies of misperception. This leads to our misnaming one another, creating a frame of language and designation that defines people and relationships. Further it permits us both to act unjustly and to tolerate injustice, unreflectively convinced that how we see, name and act is in accord with the way things are. That pattern creates and perpetuates injustice. Long before the heinous face of racism, oppression, genocide or torture shows itself, distance, difference, disregard and disdain have been etched into our hearts.

Our failure to love God and our neighbor means we can cultivate passivity toward injustice. We begin with the loves we have at hand, loves far smaller, far more manageable and far more prejudiced when we are defining reality our way rather than God's. We foster the well-being of ourselves and those we love, and we let go of the rest.

TOWARD A NEW HEART

What can throw this passivity into crisis is an encounter with Jesus Christ who tears "down the dividing wall" (Eph 2:14) and seeks to transform our hearts to love like God's. That depth of transformation is not what we want. We might welcome a more acute conscience and a little deeper compassion. But easy does it, right? It must be admitted, of course, that Christian people and churches have a major stake in the perpetuation of social Darwinism, whether of a kinder, gentler type or of the more conquering type. Wherever we may be on the spectrum, we all have a stake in the status quo. That stasis has been built on social assumptions that perpetuate perceptions and actions of injustice.

Worship—waking up to life in God in Christ for the world—is the Bible's word for what should expose our heart's complicity with injustice and motivate our transformation to live differently. In the Bible's framework, only in the context of worship is life, including injustice, so reframed that the dividing wall of hostility is torn down and our capacity to see, name and act justly is restored by God's grace. It's the transformation of the heart.

> **Reflection.** *What particular worship acts are you doing in order to open yourself up to a new heart? To a just heart? How do personal and corporate worship help this transformation? What further steps do you feel you need to take to see your heart share more of the taxonomy of compassion and action that is true of God's heart?*

HOLY WORSHIP

Whenever we worship God, we do so with language. Often verbal language, but always with language, silent or spoken. We name God, the world around us, ourselves in our worship by our voices and bodies, our ritual and spontaneity, our hearts and lips, our words and sighs.

When we name God "holy" we think of purity, and that seems like a heavenly version of Mr. Clean. But meanwhile, we are dust and to dust we shall return. So it's hard to be clean.

All this, however, takes an unexpected turn in Jesus: the holy, clean God shows up dressed in dust. Dust-like-us dust. But then you hear Jesus say in the Sermon on the Mount that we are meant to be holy as God is holy, perfect as God is perfect.

Perfect dust? Or perfect, and no longer dust?

We might think that it's not real dust. Then we are told that the crowds were astonished when Jesus taught them as one who had authority, and not like the scribes and Pharisees.

But then Jesus came down the mountain, talked to and then healed and touched a leper. So much for clean dust. The One who was said to be clean actually touched a person who was unclean as an expression of what *clean* really meant and didn't mean.

So much for Jesus as God's cleanest dust. Unless it was by touching the leper that Jesus showed us what kind of cleanliness, holiness and purity matters to God. It's a cleanliness of the heart; a compassionate, engaged will; a suffering, encountering love so real and so compelling that it draws us into the dirt of life as the only place we can actually live in a holy way. "Be clean" means to be dirty as only Jesus teaches us to be.

When Christians go to Mexico to build houses, they encounter God in the dirt of it all. When they show up for forgotten people in the inner city, it may not smell good. When they develop honest enough friendships in such settings, they learn that the aroma of their own life isn't neutral or savory all the time either. Sometimes it takes being in the smelliest or dirtiest places to discover human dignity despite our biases, God's presence amid the poor. This is why holy worship encompasses holy love and justice.

Reflection. To develop a heart like God's requires exercise. We have to give and use our heart for our heart muscle to grow in capacity and endurance. We have to give ourselves beyond ourselves. What sustained relationship or commitment of love to a marginalized, poor or vulnerable person are you or could you be committed to in this way? What will you do? Who might be your exercise partner?

JUSTICE IS IN THE NAME OF JESUS

> At the name of Jesus every knee should bend, in heaven and on earth and under the earth, and every tongue should confess that Jesus Christ is Lord, to the glory of God the Father. (Phil 2:10-11)

Eternal worship is life in the name of Jesus. Everyone and everything will bow before the Lord and all relationships in creation and the new creation will be rightly ordered. "And this is eternal life, that they may know you, the only true God, and Jesus Christ whom you have sent" (Jn 17:3).

To some this may sound like religious domination. In New Testament terms it is simply life in reality, freedom and joy. It spells the end of all forms of false and abusive power or loyalty. It is the end of what undermines our heart's longings and our broadest community.

If this communion is our eternity, then life here and now is meant to take its lead from that hope and future, understanding and practicing affirmation of the kingdom that Jesus established, the kingdom that God will one day bring to fulfillment.

The name of Jesus is what names us—as we are, in every dimension of our being, without shade or prejudice, without isolation or invisibility. We are named in Jesus in ways that validate who we are and who we are not.

When we watch the Jesus of the Gospels transform lives by gracious truth-telling, we get a foretaste of how surprising, if not shocking, Jesus' renaming will be, not least for those injustice has so wrongly named. "I never thought I would be so truly seen and named" was the message of the woman at the well (Jn 4). Many, many others share that same grace.

The biblical purpose in the revelation of this ultimate reality is not to breed passivity now but to shape life today in light of the fact that this is creation's kingdom future. This marshals the energy of our mission, sets the course for what we are going to do, tells us about what matters, distinguishes the tribe from the kingdom, and makes this the priority and not that. We recognize the urgent. We are able to define the essential.

If life in the name of Jesus is our future, it is our life and liberty, it is the grace and justice to which every day is meant to be offered. This is the worship we have been made for and will one day enter fully; it is what tells us whom we are to seek and what we are to do today.

> **Reflection.** *How does the name of Jesus instruct me to name my neighbor and myself? Who is someone that treats you like an enemy or you see as an enemy? In either direction, how does naming the other person in Jesus' name change how you see and respond? Does this practically help? If so, how? If not, why not?*

WORSHIP AS REPERCEIVING

To love the Lord our God with all our heart, mind and strength is essential to loving our neighbors as ourselves. We will be able to sustain doing the second only if we do the first. And if we fully do the first, we will do the second.

By coming to see God (even if "through a glass darkly") I can actually see myself and my neighbor more clearly. The Shema affirms, "Hear, O Israel: The LORD is our God, the LORD alone. You shall love the LORD your God with all your heart, and with all your soul, and with all your might" (Deut 6:4-5). This means in maintaining our satisfying focus on God we have less chance of projecting divine expectations on anyone or anything else. The dim glass is clear enough to know God alone is God.

This radical, clarifying, centering vision of God is the heart of Christian worship. It's the start and end of a reperceiving life. Wisdom and justice depend on it.

A gift of growing up in mountain territory in the Northwest, as I did, is that you could place yourself in the world with relative confidence. The mountains could tell you where you were and where you weren't. They could serve as a compass, a signpost. They were a comfort.

We live in a time when a confluence of postmodern factors have left many people with lost confidence that human beings can have a true sense of perspective and context. Because there is no neutral place to stand and see the universe objectively, many have come to believe that we are left with a flat, horizontal world. We can therefore have no perspective whatsoever. To claim otherwise is seen as an abuse of power. When that happens, our neighbors are seen in the same plane as ourselves, from our angle and with no possibility of a true and trustworthy elevation, let alone one of transcendence.

Christian worship makes a profound claim: God transcendently sees us from a wider vision of who and how we are. The revelation of God's power, character, creativity, compassion, attentiveness and promise makes the clear claim that God is not like us, nor are we like God. Further, both we and our neighbors have meaning and value, complexity and problems, which are bound up with the God-given capacities of being made in God's image.

Our story is not finally our own. Our life is not our own. We "live and move and have our being" because of God. We are the treasure of God's design. God is not just another perspective.

Worship gives us the chance to be taken up the mountain to see differently, more accurately, than we can otherwise do. This was precisely Martin Luther King Jr.'s point in his "I Have a Dream" speech on the steps of the Lincoln Memorial. What he saw as he looked out at the throngs of people was so much more than a political movement. He saw the people, their future and their hope because he had God's perspective. He had "been to the mountain," and it transformed how he saw everything else.

This is meant to be the typical fruit of Christian worship: we are to live in the valley with vision from the mountain. It changes how we live and love. It redefines what we can see and do. The shadow lines fall in different places. Where there had been only shadows is now sight. What had been hidden is visible. What had seemed small may now be much bigger, and what may have seemed big might now be much smaller.

Worship exposes the distortions of personal and societal sin that undergird all injustice. Worship recasts and humbles all forms of human power, which are key to what subverts human relationships and well-being. Worship delivers us from the need to make our neighbors in our image rather than to see and value them as already made in the image of God. Worship searches my stake in a world of my own making and meaning; it unmasks my self-interest, pettiness and hardness of heart. Worship reminds me that we are delivered from this otherwise hopeless, stymied place by the rescue of One who sees justly.

Worship heals us from the tragic myopia of our misperception and then sends us out into the world to love God, our neighbors and ourselves with lives that show we have seen God and therefore we see all else differently.

This side of things and that side of things turn out to be temporary human fictions, lies, crippling distinctions that the kingdom wants to break down and reorder. Barriers of difference and distinction only mirror what God seeks in Christ to draw together in one new people. God's grace tears down the dividing wall of hostility and calls us into a new community centered in God's *shalom*. When every knee is bowed and every tongue confesses that Jesus Christ is Lord, we will be a worshiping community that sees face to face. We will be changed as we see and are seen.

Reflection. *How has this book stimulated your awareness of your need to reperceive yourself? Your neighbor? God? What progress has been made as a result? What further steps do you want to take to keep changing? Who is accompanying you as a brother or sister in this effort? Write a letter to God and to a close friend about what you are coming to perceive and the ways you hope this will continue.*

WORSHIP AS RENAMING

If worship means dwelling in and living out the character of God in the world, then worship will include not only reperceiving the world but renaming it as well.

In communal worship, the gathered community practices the taxonomy of God's heart. The Word that calls and invites, comforts and assures, defines and measures, forgives and includes, heals and reminds, exhorts and commands is the Word that commissions and sends. This is the deep grammar, the revisionist naming, that we are meant to internalize and practice.

Referring to worship, John Calvin affirmed it is an act of Word and Spirit. In other words, it is both linguistic and supralinguistic. It includes the vocabulary of God and the power of God. It involves looking at those our hearts call "strangers" and hearing in Jesus' word that they are brothers, sisters, friends. In all aspects of our communal worship we are relanguaging our lives with the good news.

Like any language learning, it takes practice and review. It will mean awkwardness and failure. It will mean breaking old habits and overcoming embarrassments. It will mean taking risks. It will mean having to admit that the language we are trying to learn is first outside us, and only gradually comes to belong to us. It takes time for it to come out of the heart. It starts on our lips, engages our minds, but must eventually emerge from our heart.

Every day we are meant to come back to the gospel's Rosetta Stone, on which we find inscribed the personal, societal, and biblical languages about any given person, moment or event. The language of God's word doesn't say the same things with different words and grammar; it sees and names the same things out of different visions and relationships. We start with the language(s) we have had drummed into us by our backgrounds. But the goal of "taking every thought captive to Christ" means moving toward the Rosetta Stone of the heart of God.

The Bible is the bedrock from which we learn the taxonomy of God's heart. In both Old and New Testaments we give ear to God's Word. Like any language, we have to listen carefully to know what is God's voice and what isn't. The leaders and the community of God's people can be ventriloquists, imposing their voices where God's belongs. They and we can readily put in God's mouth the language of our hearts, not that of God's. Here again, language learning is hard work that takes time, discernment and critique.

That the people of God could impose into God's mouth the legitimacy of slavery, for example, is horrifying evidence that the deep grammar and naming of our faith can be wrong. In this, and in many other instances, we claim that our heart's language is God's and in doing so we are blasphemous and unjust.

The taxonomy of God's heart is a foreign language for us all. No one is a native speaker. We all have the capacity, but it will be harder for some. We have to want to learn. We have to believe that it is needed and worthwhile, a sufficient language for life. The goal is not some spiritual Esperanto, a shared but foreign amalgam of sounds and words. It is more like a shared grammar of the heart that gains varied expressions.

I have a couple of English-speaking American friends who are also fluent in Italian. They are very verbal people, warmly and easily expressive in words and actions. Each was drawn to Italian culture, art and language. Though they live and work daily in an English-speaking world, Italian is always lurking underneath. Not infrequently, they will insert an Italian phrase that more nearly captures the spirit of what they want to communicate. I have never seen either of them in uninhibited Italian conversation, though I would love to. If and when I ever have that chance, I am quite sure of what I will see: though I will not understand the words they are speaking, I will understand and experience both of them more near to their true selves than I have done so far.

In gospel terms this is what it means to live renaming the world with the taxonomy, the grammar, the vocabulary and the names of the kingdom of God. In this language of God's heart we will find we are more fully ourselves than we have ever been—and so will our neighbor.

The challenge is that we don't easily believe this. We don't find God's language intuitive or natural, because it's not. That's why we need worship and why we dare not cease our practicing. We will need mentors, conversation partners, teachers. We have to practice in the classroom, but also in the streets. We have to learn to make it our own, so it gradually comes out of our heart.

Reflection. How have the thoughts and stories of this book stimulated your awareness of your need to rename yourself? Your neighbor? God? What progress has been made as a result? What further steps do you want to take to keep changing? Who is accompanying you as a brother or sister in this effort? Continue your letter to God and to a close friend about how you are practicing renaming, and the ways you hope this will continue. What difference do you hope it will make?

WORSHIP AS REACTING

Worship must be performed—embodied. Only then is it the worship God seeks. The performative nature of worship is not only or primarily about what happens when we are in a gathered service, but when we walk into all the rest of our lives and into our complex world. Though not as sequential as this implies, the movement is like a spiral from reperceiving to renaming to reacting. Each flows out of worship. No part can be left out. No part is dispensable. No part is autonomous.

Worship includes the messiness of jumping in wherever and however we are able to do so. Gathered-worship leadership, which is intrinsically engaged in all these dimensions, can fan the wind of the Holy Spirit in helping those present to participate in this rich vocation.

The preacher has the vital role of focusing attention on ways Scripture calls God's people to renewed perception, naming and acting. The preacher needs to be a witness to this threefold call and transformation in her or his own life, and to help the congregation embrace these as dimensions of their calling. Then the pastor-leader needs to enable the congregation as a community to find ways to practice reperceiving, renaming and reacting. Out of this some in the community are drawn to ordinary and some into more extraordinary settings in which that vocation can be carried out.

Barbara is a woman in Berkeley with a heart that can reach out. She is not someone readily made for intrepid international travel in war zones, but she cares and suffers with people she has heard about but not met. Among these are women in the Goma region of eastern Congo who have suffered severe physical and sexual brutality. The viciousness of soldiers and militia in that area has caused a dramatic incidence of fistula, where women have been so sexually brutalized that they are left incontinent. This leads to shame as well as to eviction from their homes and villages.

Through no fault of their own, these women are seen as worthless embarrassments to their family and their community. They are literally treated as dead, left without place, people or things. They are without hope in the world.

This story is changed for some because of the remarkable ministry of the HEAL Africa hospital in Goma. This Christian hospital serves these women and does everything in its power to provide the care and surgeries necessary to help them rebuild their lives. Barbara's family and friends include people who have been the bridge to HEAL Africa, and who have enabled Barbara to see and carry in her heart the profound isolation of these women. Barbara's vision is to give to each of the many women who come to HEAL Africa a fine handmade quilt to help them know they are seen, valued and loved. This has expanded into the gathering of hundreds of quilts from around the San Francisco Bay Area, to send to HEAL Africa.

When the quilts were gathered, the First Presbyterian Church of Berkeley wanted to commission them as a blanket of God's comforting presence and healing love. We drape them over the pews in our sanctuary. We invited the congregation to wrap themselves in these expressions of God's beauty and love, and in silence to imagine a woman who faces that kind of desperation. We asked the congregation to imagine those women wrapped in a dignifying, loving embrace. Then we prayed together a prayer that sought to see, name and love them justly.

These acts of worship are, in that moment and in their lingering impact, a small part of an embodiment of a God who longs for all things to be new. I don't think we are the same people after we have been shrouded by these quilts and lifted up the names of the unseen, the discarded, the repellent. By God's grace, worship is doing its work.

What mission of justice do you believe God wants you to take up? Will you do so? How? When? Where? With whom?

> **Reflection.** *How has this book stimulated your awareness of your need to react in relation to yourself? Your neighbor? God? What progress has been made as a result? What further steps do you want to take to keep changing? Who is accompanying you as a brother or sister in this effort? Continue your letter to God and to a close friend about how you are practicing reacting and the ways you hope this will continue. What difference do you hope it will make?*

MOVING DAY

Today is moving day.

This move is not like packing a U-Haul. What's being moved is not nearly as discrete nor as easily manipulated. Neither can it be accomplished by hiring someone else to do the heavy lifting or by rousting friends to show up early Saturday morning. It's not a quick move or an easy one.

This move requires unusual commitment and dedication. It means deciding that the social universe we are nurtured to inhabit is something we are prepared to examine carefully and seek release from, as we refocus our hearts and minds. The faint-hearted will have a difficult time getting over the threshold of social energy that resists such a move, but it is a necessary part of the process.

This move is an act of humility, a laying down of our assumptions and preferences, a readiness to believe that someone else's life makes a decisive claim on our own. That is not the American Dream. It is the kingdom of God.

This move involves us more than it involves our stuff. It's a personal move, internal and external, spiritual and physical. It's a move that happens from the inside but has to show up on the outside or no real move has happened. It should be clear from concrete actions and uncommon instincts that we are living on a larger stage and for the sake of others whose lives are at the margins. What's more, we do this because they are now among our people; the world of *them* has become part of the world of *us*. We could no more neglect responding to their circumstances than we could our family.

It's not a move in a straight line. It's a move that undulates, wobbles and slips. This should come as no surprise because so many things are changing at one time. We are establishing a new center of gravity that is no longer only about our own balance.

It's not a move in isolation either. It's a move that will inevitably be affected by others. If we think we are the only ones making the move, we will probably not do so, or not for long. We are choosing to live out a different sociology, ordering the passions and delights of our hearts in accordance with that. This new social world will take us to different places and put us in previously unlikely relationships.

This move will mean pain because we are going to be entering circumstances that can expose us to the desperation, violence and neglect that many people experience daily. Yet this is also why such a move can be the way we step into greater experiences of joy, the discovery in the midst of suffering that God is powerfully present as Maker, Rescuer and Healer. Grace always gives, especially in the midst of need. It turns out that the lives of the poor and marginalized, of victims and sufferers are wider than we would have otherwise imagined.

Moving from the world of *them* to the world of *us* is a move further into the heart of God. That is finally why this move is also for any who claim to be followers of Jesus Christ. This is not an optional side tour, a temporary distraction. It's a move that the Bible depicts as a move home. It's where we all were meant to live, where we are no longer fooled into thinking that the divisions we are so accustomed to are final or true. When we get home we realize home is a bigger, better, more just and more loving a place than we might have dared to dream.

Of course, all this makes it a dangerous move. Things won't be as they have been. Vestiges of small-heartedness will have to die. Defiant parochialism will get snuffed out. Life on this side of things won't draw or satisfy us in the same way. The buzz over the nickel-plated faucets will seem silly. Justice for our tribe only will no longer seem like justice, because it's not. This dangerous move is God's invitation into faithful worship. We love the Lord our God with all our heart, mind, soul and strength, and our neighbor as ourselves. That is why we are. This is how we are to live—seeking a just hope.

Today—everyday—is moving day.

Sabbath Encouragement

Again, we need to pause, especially since we are committed to act. Fatigue, burnout and paralysis are always knocking on our doors.

The rhythm of sustainable Christian action comes from rest: from living in the rest or sabbath of God whose actions create and re-create us. We love because God first loved us. It's true, faith must be walked to be faith. Grace does not make action optional. It makes action compelling and possible. But we know that our acts are neither themselves the source of grace nor ever adequate enough as an expression of our own gratitude, let alone as a response to human need. We need to drink in God's grace and take the long view precisely so we can sustain our action by remembering who we are and who we are not, and by remembering that our acts are framed by God's supreme act of hope in Christ:

> Therefore, since we are justified by faith, we have peace with God through our Lord Jesus Christ, through whom we have obtained access to this grace in which we stand; and we boast in our hope of sharing the glory of God. And not only that, but we also boast in our sufferings, knowing that suffering produces endurance, and endurance produces character, and character produces hope, and hope does not disappoint us, because God's love has been poured into our hearts through the Holy Spirit that has been given to us.
>
> For while we were still weak, at the right time Christ died for the ungodly. Indeed, rarely will anyone die for a righteous person—though perhaps for a good person someone might actually dare to die. But God proves his love for us in that while we still were sinners Christ died for us. Much more surely then, now that we have been justified by his blood, will we be saved through him from the wrath of God. For if while we were enemies, we were reconciled to God through the death of his Son, much more surely, having been recon-

ciled, will we be saved by his life. But more than that, we even boast in God through our Lord Jesus Christ, through whom we have now received reconciliation. (Rom 5:1-11)

1. I urge you to meditate on and savor what Christ has already done for the salvation and transformation of the world—including you. It turns out you and I are not the saviors of the world, nor do we need to be.

2. I urge you to remember that we live in the assurance that God is the initiator of action that will one day enable the lion to lie down with the lamb. We are joining God's action that seeks to establish the justice and shalom of the kingdom.

3. I urge you to remember God alone is infinite, all-present, all-loving and everlasting. You and I are finite and fallen. This does not let us off the hook, but it certainly should calibrate our expectations.

4. I urge you to practice remembering and celebrating this good news daily in your personal worship, and weekly as you gather with God's people to worship. Lose this, and the weight of what we are talking about here will crush you. Practice it and you can, by grace, carry it with joy.

PRAYER

We bind to ourselves this day
The power of God to hold and lead,
his eye to watch, his might to stay,
his ear to harken to my need:
the wisdom of my God to teach,
his hand to guide, his shield to ward:
the word of God to give me speech,
his heavenly host to be my guard.

Christ be with us, Christ before us,
Christ behind us, Christ deep within us,
Christ below us, Christ above us,
Christ at our right hand, Christ at our left hand,
Christ as we lie down, Christ as we arise,
Christ as we stand,
Christ in the heart of everyone who thinks of us and everyone we
    think of,
Christ in the mouth of everyone who speaks of us, and everyone
    we speak of,
Christ in every eye we see with,
Christ in every ear we hear with.

St. Patrick's Breastplate (adapted)

Conclusion

Just Hope

Of all the chapters of hope in the Bible, Romans 8 has most often and most deeply spoken to me. This chapter is one of the apostle Paul's micro-to-macro texts: from the heart to the heavens, nothing and no one will be untouched by God's redemptive plan. Paul is full and overflowing with confidence with what *is*, matched with pastoral and theological acknowledgment of what is *yet to be*.

The One who has drawn near in Jesus Christ is the One who changes even today, such that Paul can say with faithful confidence, "there is therefore now no condemnation for those who are in Christ Jesus" (Rom 8:1). And at the same time, Paul admits that we await tomorrow, for "the sufferings of this present time are not worth comparing with the glory about to be revealed to us. For the creation waits with eager longing" (Rom 8:18-19) for what has not yet happened. We live in between.

This book is about seeking justice in between. We must seek justice because we live in between what God has created and begun but not yet finished. (Justice is therefore not yet complete.) We can only do this by seeking what we do not yet see fully or clearly. (Justice is therefore a hope.)

For Paul, life in between is our hope, not a reason for our despair. By God's acts of faithfulness we long for the very thing God will bring to fulfillment. We groan in our waiting, but we groan with hope. And we invest in the waiting process one of the most valuable contributions we could possibly make: faith in God who through Jesus Christ and by the Holy Spirit is bringing and will bring all things to consummation.

The experience of waiting is expected. The assurance in our waiting is the faithfulness that God has already shown and the consummation to which Jesus himself pointed. Paul writes, "For in hope we were saved. Now hope that is seen is not hope. For who hopes for what is seen? But if we hope for what we do not see, we wait for it with patience" (Rom 8:24-25).

While we wait, we have work to do. For if the seedbed of injustice is the human heart, the even more powerful seedbed of new hearts is nothing less than the life of the triune God in whom we are to dwell. Hope is born out of this divine seedbed and, ultimately, of the fruit for which we long.

We are not alone in this. Paul points out, "the Spirit helps us in our weakness; for we do not know [for example] how to pray as we ought, but that very Spirit intercedes with sighs too deep for words. And God, who searches the heart, knows what is the mind of the Spirit, because the Spirit intercedes for the saints according to the will of God" (Rom 8:26-27).

Then we hear one of the toughest and also one of the best statements in the New Testament:

We know that all things [in this long waiting] work together for good for those who love God, who are called according to his purpose. For those whom he foreknew he also predestined to be conformed to the image of his Son, in order that he might be the firstborn within a large family. And those whom he predestined he also called; and those whom he called he also justified; and those whom he justified he also glorified. (Rom 8:28-30)

The full theological sweep of these brief verses is beyond our consideration at the moment. What seems most pertinent, however, is the overriding confidence that even all of what is now so tragically and horribly wrong in the world, including all of the darkest and most pernicious forms of injustice, will in the providence and purpose of God come to their right end, namely, to be remade to mirror the reality, the glory, of God's own life and character. The greatest hope for the human heart is the heart of God.

Staggered by this, Paul then exudes:

What then are we to say about these things? If God is for us, who is against us? He who did not withhold his own Son, but gave him up for all of us, will he not with him also give us everything else? Who will bring any charge against God's elect? It is God who justifies. Who is to condemn? It is Christ Jesus, who died, yes, who was raised, who is at the right hand of God, who indeed intercedes for us. Who will separate us from the love of Christ? Will hardship, or distress, or persecution, or famine, or nakedness, or peril, or sword? As it is written,

"For your sake we are being killed all day long;
    we are accounted as sheep to be slaughtered."

No, in all these things we are more than conquerors through him who loved us. For I am convinced that neither death, nor life, nor angels, nor rulers, nor things present, nor things to come, nor powers, nor height, nor depth, nor anything else in all creation, will be able to separate us from the love of God in Christ Jesus our Lord. (Rom 8:31-39)

So, is all this effort of seeking a just hope a work of fiction? Our lives are meant to answer no. Vigorously. Actively. Persistently. But even more profoundly and importantly, the gospel of Jesus Christ pronounces the final no. God has acted to redeem and restore, to bring justice and to establish a kingdom without abuse of power toward anyone or anything any more; and that will be the final word. The apostle therefore marshals all the language at his command to affirm the trustworthiness of this hope and the joyful anticipation that no other perception, name or act in this world or the next will exceed the love and purposes of God.

But what is the evidence of this in our world today? Paul says it's that you and I live this hope. May we then live this just hope, and may it be the reality that unmasks every other. May this just hope change our heart to be more like God's, as we wait for the day when "justice [will] roll down like waters, and righteousness like an ever-flowing stream" (Amos 5:24). That's God dream. It is what's coming, and that is no fiction.

Group Discussion Guide

The material placed within the chapters from section to section is designed for individual reflection. To create a group process, I encourage you to walk back through each of the sections that appear within the chapters, discussing your responses with one another. These sections are copied here for your convenience. There are also some questions added to enhance your group process. This book is meant to be gently, if persistently, applied. Encourage one another, pray for each other, and seek God's loving transformation.

CHAPTER 1: OUR ADDRESS

What words capture your social and spiritual location in the world? Which do you think are the most influential in your life? Which do you think most affect others you encounter? Why? What observations do these factors lead you to make?

It's All Good (Over Here)

What things do you experience or assume every day are part of life on this side of things? Prioritize the top five things for you. How would you respond if three of these things were indefinitely, even permanently, removed from your life? How would you define life in those circumstances? Compare notes on these answers and reasons.

It's What It Is (Over There)

What would be the biggest differences in life if you lived on that other side of things? What if hope meant survival, not improvement or alleviation of daily problems? Would your prayers change? How do others in your small group answer these questions? What patterns, if any, do you notice in one another's answers?

If You Just Keep Moving

How does your life's momentum affect your capacity for empathy: entering into the lives and needs of others, especially those who have no tie or evident benefit to your life? Notice today or this week the time and energy you devote to engage with the needs of others. Does empathy cost you? How do you feel about that price? How do answers in your small group compare with one another?

CHAPTER 2: PAYING ATTENTION TO PAYING ATTENTION

The "We"

Who are in your concentric circles of "we"? What typical signals tell you that someone is "your people"? What tells you they are not "your people"? Why? What makes someone or others "they"? What observations can you make of these distinctions? What do they tell you about your heart? Are you close to any or many you consider "they"?

It's Plain as Fact

What moments or circumstances expose your distance, fear, rejection, anger, prejudice, dislike of "they"? Why do these responses seem natural and justified? What experiences or voices in your life have contributed to that? In your small group, what similarities and differences do you find in discussing these issues of "theyness"?

Not a Problem

Do you invest energy daily in avoiding problems or pain—in your life and in the lives of those you love? In the lives of those you work with? What does this lead you to see in your heart? Who is someone you know who does a good job of stepping toward the needs of others? Why do you think so?

What's Inside Is Outside

Write a letter to God about your heart in relation to your life in a world of suffering and injustice. Try to explain to God the current state of your heart and the changes you think would be needed to make your heart like God's. Do you desire this change? How will you pray for it? Who in your life could help encourage you in this change? How could you ask them to help?

Chapter 3: The Problem of Misperceiving

How Misperception Shapes Self-Perception

Consider in these next days all the varied ways you perceive the people in the world around you, near and far. What lenses are you using? Why? How do they affect others and what you see about them? When and where do you see those around you, or in other places in the world, as merely a means? Why do you do so? If the tragic headline referred to your sibling or close friend, how differently would you respond?

Injustice Rolls Down

If justice means "to make things right," what is one area of injustice that especially matters to you (or, alternatively, one that you think should matter to you but doesn't yet)? Write down ten to fifteen things you could do in the next couple of months to enlarge your understanding and empathy for people in that circumstance. What do you think God's heart feels in response to them? What about yours? If you are in a small group, how could you help one another follow through on these intentions?

CHAPTER 4: LEARNING TO SEE

The Broken Image

What mirrors have you most trusted to show you your image? In what ways have these mirrors told the truth? Told lies? How do they affect the capacity you have to see yourself and to see others?

Seeing as We Are Seen

Make a list of how you think some of the most important people in your life see you. What do most people who think they see you truly manage to get wrong or fail to see? Why? How influential for you are the views these people hold of you? How do their opinions affect your life? How do their opinions of you in turn affect how you see others?

Seeing in Ordinary

How acute is your attention to the world of need around you? To things and people beyond your immediate concern or attention? In what ways are you and are you not a person who actively pays attention to more than your circumstances as you walk through life each day? When you look back on the last forty-eight hours, what details of life and people not your own can you list? Describe someone you know who is strong in this kind of attentiveness. How do you respond to their example?

Vision Versus Sight

Sight is how you see. Vision is how you see *and* your interpretation of what you see. What factors most significantly affect your vision of people around you? Of people in need? Of global suffering? Of individuals who are victims of violence and oppression? In your group, after discussing these questions, talk about what you have learned from one another about your "vision" by listening to each other.

Chapter 5: Self-Seeing

My Own Broken Mirror

What has cracked or broken your mirror? Why? What has the impact been? How has the grace of God helped you face this and seek God's renewing change in your own life, and in your capacity to mirror the worth of others to them? In your group, talk about your own experiences with cracked mirrors and then discuss how knowing about one another's cracked mirrors affects how you see and love each other.

Beyond the Social Bell Curve

What is the bell curve of your social relationships? What type of people fit where in your social awareness? Draw a bell curve of those who matter in your social environment and those who matter to the kingdom of God. How similar and different are these lists? Why?

The Bible and the Broken Mirror

How does this theme in the Bible help you see yourself? What common or different threads strike you? Why? Do you see yourself as an insider or an outsider to the Bible's portrait of our brokenness? Why?

Share this in your small group and prayer for one another.

Chapter 6: The Crux

Compassionate Dispassion

Our perceiving can be done from such safe distances that the needs of others make no claim on us. This is part of our lives of privilege. What are the evidences of privilege in your life, especially in your assumptions? What are examples of how privilege shapes your life at this point? Why does it matter to try to understand how basic and different it is to live with privilege? What do you think Jesus says about privilege? What does privilege prevent us from seeing or feeling? Why?

Salty Memories

In what ways have you come near to people in pain or injustice? How have such situations affected you? How penetrating or heart-changing were those experiences? How do they or don't they daily shape your heart?

What do other members of your small group have to contribute to each other by way of their own experiences?

Matters of Identity

My identity matters to me far more than my neighbor's. Fair enough. But why does our suffering neighbors' identity matter so little to us? Why is it so discretionary that we are very slow, even passive, in responding to their crisis? What is it about my identity that lets me live so comfortably with such dissonance and need? Is this similar or different for others in your small group?

Field of Vision

If no one sees with full clarity, what do you look for in the faces of others? How hard or easy is it for you to read signs of the pain in others' lives? How do you respond when you see it? What does it take for you to open your heart to them and their need? What do you make of that fact?

Depth Perception

Choose one primary global issue of need (e.g., Israel-Palestine, Congo, Pakistan-India, child slavery, bonded labor, sex trafficking) or choose one person you have contact with who is at the margins of justice (e.g., a homeless person, a panhandler, etc.). Track this area's or person's needs daily through whatever means you can (conversation, personal visits, Internet, prayer, books, reflection, imagination, etc.). How deep are you willing to go in entering another person's reality and need? What stops you? Paralyzes you?

The Key to My Neighbor's House

How do you respond to Neuffer's statement "What's most chilling when you meet a murderer is that you meet yourself"? Do you find yourself instinctively accepting or denying that statement? Why? Do you find the horrors of others imaginable within your heart?

Share this in your small group and compare notes with one another's response. What sense does this make to you as a group?

Dimness

How are you encouraged by God's desire to help you see and respond to our world less dimly? Do you like seeing more clearly and brightly? What are the costs? How can this journey for you be helped by others doing the same?

CHAPTER 7: CHOOSING NAMES

Renaming Dustin

Let yourself imagine being Dustin. Describe your life if you lived it in Dustin's circumstances. What would your heart, mind, soul be like? Why? Where would you turn for help? Whom would you rely on to tell you who you are? Why?

Wrong Names

Take steps to become deliberately conscious of the labels and names you are inwardly and quietly, or outwardly and publicly, assigning to people you see, especially those who are in situations of need, suffering, pain, isolation. If possible, make daily, even hourly lists for a week or so of all the names you internally or externally give others. Try changing the names you ascribe to someone and see how it changes your perception of them.

The Story of Naming and Misnaming

In ordinary life, our naming neglects, forgets and abuses God's way of naming. What are examples of that in your life this week? What happens or doesn't happen when you misname someone, that is, give them a name that they don't deserve and that diminishes them in your sight or in others'? Are you aware of doing this?

How aware are others around you? How aware are those you are misnaming?

Do We Hear Ourselves?

When you see others being misnamed, what is your internal response? Do you tend to identify with the misnamer or the misnamed? Why? What do you do about this if the person misnamed is present? Is not present? Are the responses similar or different? How do you wish you would respond? What would it take for you to make that kind of response?

What would it take for others in your small group to change in your misnaming?

CHAPTER 8: A NEW NAME

Life in the Name

In what ways is this biblical theme of naming and renaming familiar to you? Is it part of how you think about your own life as a disciple? How do you experience being named or renamed by God? What does this theme of naming mean to you personally? To how you name others in your life? Why? How has your name been changed by the name of Jesus in your life?

How about others in your group?

Taxonomy of God's Heart

Over these weeks, where are you seeing God's taxonomy of heart becoming more familiar to you and more fully your own? How is this happening? What spiritual practices are most helpful in nurturing this new heart? Where is your heart most responsive? Most resistant to these changes? If paying more for fair-trade products cuts into your budget, for example, would you or do you make that choice?

Share these things in your small group as candidly as you are willing to do, and encourage one another in this process.

CHAPTER 9: SOCIAL NAMING

The Justice and Injustice of Naming

How have you experienced being wrongly named by someone in authority or power in your life? How did you feel? How did or does it still affect you? Who is someone you have wrongly named? What do you think has been the impact of that for them? Is it possible for this to be changed?

What experiences have others in your small group had in this area?

Naming and Power

Recall one of the most significant experiences of misnaming in your life or that of someone else (known to you personally or that you have known in some way). What happened? What was the impact? Why? How do you feel about that experience? What does it lead you to conclude about the power of misnaming?

A Flair

Notice today the social naming going on around you in various settings. What were some of the names? What caused them to be assigned? How fair or unfair is that to any of the individuals involved? Have you ever been socially misnamed in a way that caused a crisis for you? Why? What was it? How did you respond?

What about others in your small group?

Cool Guy

Think of someone you know or observe or know about whose external name is not their internal one. Why is there this difference? Why and how does it matter? How do you respond to the dissonance between the two?

Are there some in your small group who might also share their experience of being misnamed or of misnaming? What has been the impact and why?

Linguistic Management

What euphemisms do you notice yourself using when you know or acknowledge underneath a darker name for someone you dislike, disdain, judge? From where do those perceptions and names come? To what sorts of traits or actions in someone else are they most likely to attach? Do you believe they are justified? What would the other person say in response?

CHAPTER 10: DISTORTED NAMES

Butter and Cream

Do you have any close friendships with people of another race or class from your own? Can you think of a relationship you have had in which the racial and class distinction between you and the other person suddenly became an issue between you? How did it happen? Why? How did it affect each of you? How did you rename yourself or each other?

Disabled Hearts

What, if any, painful memories of being misnamed have you experienced in your life or seen in the lives of others that prohibit you from being who you are? From using your gifts? From expressing your freedom? What has been the impact? What does it take to reverse the damage and to set the name right?

Harami

Stigma can be excruciating. What stigmas, if any, have you ever been assigned or assigned to others with no choice of your own or of theirs? What are the most distressing ones you have experienced or witnessed (e.g., gender, race, intelligence, physical disability, class, skill, etc.)? What stigmas do you hear relegating people to neglect most readily and easily? Why?

Share these impressions in your small group. What do you find are the common threads? The distinctions?

Chapter 11: Changing Names

You are probably not a Dalit, yet we live in a world of Dalits of many kinds, and we do little to change that reality. We live in a world of daily gender, racial, class and physical injustice perpetrated all around us. What signs of these patterns are you seeing this week? How do they help make people targets? How and why are they so easily doled out toward others?

A Contagion of the Heart

Why are names like the N-word so hard to bury? What "N-words" have you had used against you? What makes a word like that that you use to label others, or by which you feel named, degrading? Have you tried, or should you try, to bury it? Why? What has happened in that effort? What (internal or external) prompts you to use it or others to use it toward you?

Is there some way you and your small group might instigate your own burial ceremony? What name would each of you need to bury most?

Viral

What comes to you as an example of some viral name you have received or passed along that keeps you or others at the social margins where injustice is tolerated by those in power? How did or does that name spread? What does that tell you about its power and force? Its attraction and utility?

What variation do you find in your small group's experiences of these patterns?

President Obama

How do words shape what is socially or politically possible for our lives? How do they shape what is possible for the poorest of the world? What does "President Obama" represent as a change in name? What is or is not the impact of that change? What name might you seek to give to someone to help them live with freedom and dignity, justice and honor?

Passive-Aggressive

How do you feel about this history of the word *genocide?* Why? Does any other example come to mind in a parallel vein? Does this breed cynicism, resignation or some other response for you? Why? How would you feel about this if you were someone in Darfur or Croatia or if your ancestors were Armenian?

Reality-Creating

How do you find yourself or others creating reality by the words you assign to others or to circumstances? How do you do that? Why? In what ways are you using words that imprison others? Distance others? Set others free? Is this just? How has your life been created for better and worse by the names others have given you? How could you practice naming others redemptively?

True Naming

What names do you wish you had been given by someone—or something you think currently misnames you? What name do you currently use toward someone but think you need to change in order to name justly and truly? How can you do that? What will help you practice that?

CHAPTER 12: FREE TO ACT

External Evidence

How do inertia, resignation or paralysis affect your heart's readiness to "do justice" in the world? In what ways are paralysis or resignation a further act of injustice? What can break this cycle in your life or in the lives of others who could make a response but don't?

How can your small group encourage one another in this?

Face to Face

If the eternal trajectory is "face to face" with God and with one another, our lives here are to reflect and practice this. Make a map of those you see face to face. As you make a series of concentric circles, from those you see directly and clearly to those you barely see at all, what makes the difference in your sight, in your naming and in your actions of living face to face?

For God So Loved the World

If this is God's way of seeing, naming and acting, what implications are there for us in addition to our own personal salvation? If we are God's plan for showing this reality, what does it compel you to consider and to do differently in the world? Especially what will you do toward those least prone to see or know the evidence of such love and justice? Who can encourage you in this? Who can you encourage? How?

Helen and Michael

What do you learn from this story of Helen and Michael? What has it transformed? Why? What action could you take to show a similar love? Who do you not want to engage and truly see and name? If you think you should do otherwise, what are some first steps you could take?

God's Contagion of Hope

Hope is typically caught and stimulated like a healthy contagion. Does anyone exemplify living this way to you? Are you prepared to seek to live this way—to move forward to preempt negative naming and take new actions that reflect the justice and love of God?

Look back as a small group and notice the ways you have seen each other take positive steps in this direction in recent months.

An Offering of Abundance and Inadequacy

If we don't know what we see until we act on our vision, what steps are you taking to test and develop, to refine and improve your vision by acting? What bold new act for the next season of life are you sensing that God may be asking you to make for the sake of justice and mercy toward those suffering and in need?

How can your small group help to hold one another to this intention and action?

CHAPTER 13: SUFFERING

Grace upon Grace

How clearly do you think you see your own privilege? What are examples of that in your daily life? Is it racial? Cultural? Educational? Economic? These can be gifts that help us see more accurately sometimes, but they can as readily be blinders. What disciplines and actions could you take over the next few weeks to practice seeing, naming and acting less out of privilege and more out of gratitude for grace and justice?

Turning Point

Our hearts are changed when we are prepared to identify with those in need—enter, share, step inside. Are you doing this? What could be your next step? Where do you notice you get most easily stopped? Why? What do you think that tells you about the challenge of your own transformation? Are there people you know who are inspiring to you in this area of your own need?

Two Letters

Focus on some headline crisis of need in the world and personalize your relationship to the concern (e.g., "my brother in Darfur," "my cousin with AIDS in Malawi," "my friend uncharged but imprisoned in Manila"). Write your thoughts and feelings and actions and how they are changed by "my."

Share your reflections with your small group.

The Teacher

Whose suffering are you sharing at this point in your reflections?

How did that come to be so? What forms does your love take? How have you been sharing in the suffering or pain of others? How much further do you think you need to be willing to go in doing so?

CHAPTER 14: PRACTICING DIGNITY

The Call to Practice
Are you out of your chair? Where are you practicing doing justice? What are your practices showing you? How and why?

What God Sees, God Gives
Find a photograph of someone in need that especially captures your attention. Using this picture as a kind of icon of vulnerability, spend five to ten minutes each day this week meditating on the photograph. Try to imagine, feel, share in what you can infer about that person's life. What are the most difficult aspects of his or her experience for you to imagine? What is easier? Why? How would you feel if you were that individual?

CHAPTER 15: THE ACT OF WORSHIP

Toward a New Heart
What particular worship acts are you doing in order to open yourself up to a new heart? To a just heart? How does personal and corporate worship help this transformation? What further steps do you feel you need to take to see your heart share more of the taxonomy of compassion and action that is true of God's heart?

Pray for this in your small group and seek to live out the heart of God more fully.

Holy Worship
To develop a heart like God's requires exercise. We have to give and use our heart for our heart muscle to grow in capacity and endurance. We have to give ourselves beyond ourselves. What sustained relationship or commitment of love to a marginalized, poor

or vulnerable person are you or could you be committed to in this way? What will you do? Who might be your exercise partner?

Justice Is in the Name of Jesus

How does the name of Jesus instruct me to name my neighbor and myself? Who is someone that treats you like an enemy or you see as an enemy? In either direction, how does naming the other person in Jesus' name change how you see and respond? Does this practically help? If so, how? If not, why not?

Worship as Reperceiving

How has this book stimulated your awareness of your need to reperceive yourself? Your neighbor? God? What progress has been made as a result? What further steps do you want to take to keep changing? Who is accompanying you as a brother or sister in this effort? Write a letter to God and to a close friend about what you are coming to perceive and the ways you hope this will continue.

Worship as Renaming

How have the thoughts and stories of this book stimulated your awareness of your need to rename yourself? Your neighbor? God? What progress has been made as a result? What further steps do you want to take to keep changing? Who is accompanying you as a brother or sister in this effort? Continue your letter to God and to a close friend about how you are practicing renaming, and the ways you hope this will continue. What difference do you hope it will make?

Worship as Reacting

How has this book stimulated your awareness of your need to react in relation to yourself? Your neighbor? God? What progress has been made as a result? What further steps do you want to take to keep changing? Who is accompanying you as a brother or sister in this effort? Continue your letter to God and to a close friend about how you are practicing reacting and the ways you hope this will continue. What difference do you hope it will make?

What mission of justice do you believe God wants you to take up? Will you do so? How? When? Where? With whom?

Acknowledgments

Behind these pages are ideas, experiences, beliefs, convictions, perceptions, stories, fears and hopes—all expressions of influence of various kinds. Among the most significant influence are people who have touched my life, some of whom have also contributed significantly to this book.

First and foremost in this list are my wife, Janet, and our sons, Peter and Sam, to whom I dedicate this book. Their encouragement and support in this process has mattered at every stage. Without Janet's generous love and patience this book would not have been possible.

Friends who have also been important teachers in some of the themes of this book include Mary Ellen Azada, Craig Barnes, Tom Boyce, Jill Boyce, Holly Burkhalter, Susan Brady, Phillippe Daniel, Justin Dillon, Joyce French, Nathan George, Julia Jalalat, Ken Johnston, Doris Kraft, Kurt Labberton, Chris Long, Justin McRoberts, Glenn and Siobhan Miles, Halleine Morrison, Marilyn Morrison, Mitali Perkins, Joshua Ralston, Sarah Ralston, Julie Sept, Doug Stevens, Xiaosheng, Dustin Webb, Anne Webb, Don Webb, Sharon Cohn Wu, and my church family at the First Presbyterian Church of Berkeley. Also John Stott, whose life has been the story of a gospel-shaped heart.

Particularly valuable conversation partners, advisors and mentors in this project whose help refined what you will find here include Alexis Abernathy, Michael Barram, Megan Handley, Bethany Hoang, Patti Nicolson, Andrew Penner, Matt Prinz, Amy Sherman, John Yoo. Ginny Hearn's contributions were pure gift.

The joy, catalyst and encouragement of Kathy Helmers as my literary agent, as well as the fine editorial dedication and thoughtfulness of Cindy Bunch at InterVarsity Press, have each been indispensable.

Steve Hayner and Tim Dearborn continue to be friends and mentors in countless ways who, along with Gary Haugen, are heartmates and inspirations to me, especially in pursuit of God's heart for justice. Likewise, Zac Niringiye has taken me into places of compassion and understanding I could only have gone with him as my guide.

I am very grateful for the contributions of any and all friends and colleagues, but I take responsibility for this final product. I present it as offering with hope for our hearts and for justice because of the heart of God in Jesus Christ.